LIMN NUMBER THREE
SENTINEL DEVICES
Edited by Frédéric Keck and Andrew Lakoff

Preface

THE POLAR ICE CAP RAPIDLY RECEDES; colonies of honeybees collapse in alarming numbers; androgynous fish are detected in rivers and streams. These reports not only describe recent events, but also function as signs of an ominous and rapidly encroaching future. In this issue of *Limn* we focus on how this future makes its appearance in the present. Many of the threats we now find most alarming—climate change, environmental radiation, emerging disease, endocrine disrupters, toxic chemicals—are not immediately perceptible to human senses. We rely on non-human indicators, whether animals or detection devices, to alert us to their possible onset. Such indicators can be thought of as sentinels, or heralds of an approaching danger.

The term sentinel comes to us from the military world, and refers to a soldier who goes to the front in order to see whether an enemy is advancing. It is instructive to contrast the sentinel with two other figures that can be used to envision the future: the prophet and the prognosticator. The prophet is a classical figure who interprets images of an impending future through practices such as divination. Despite advanced warning, those who receive prophecies typically cannot ward off their fates. The prognosticator, in turn, is a figure from the early modern period who gathers detailed knowledge about the present in order to calculate, and plan for, what is likely to happen in the near future.

The sentinel plays a different role. This figure presents a vigilant watchfulness that can aid in preparation for an uncertain, but potentially catastrophic future. The word derives from the Latin *sentire*, to feel or sense. Thus the figure of the sentinel is bound up with both the problem of perception and the question of whether the detection of danger can successfully ward off a coming crisis. In the contemporary context of ecological anxiety, the sentinel has taken on an expanded meaning: it has come to describe living beings or technical devices that provide the first signs of an impending catastrophe. For example, a polar bear perched on a fragile piece of ice may serve as a harbinger of climate disaster; or an uptick in over-the-counter flu medication sales may indicate the onset of a deadly pandemic.

Non-human beings have served as environmental sentinels from the beginning of the industrial revolution. Most famously, canaries were brought into coal mines due to their heightened sensitivity to gas. In the late nineteenth century, botanist Wilhelm Nylander mapped air pollution in Paris by looking at lichen distribution in the Luxembourg gardens. He called the plants "hygiometers" since they could assess the salubrity of a given location. German botanists Kolkwitz and Marsson used fish in a similar way to study river pollution at the turn of the twentieth century.

A century later, while sentinel devices of various kinds have become increasingly present in domains of health and ecological threat, the meaning of their signals is often ambiguous or contested. Indeed, their efficacy in inciting action varies. In the case of climate change, for example, indicators pointing to global warming have proven able to stimulate precautionary policies (such as a or a cap-and-trade system) in some places but not others. Another example comes from disease detection: the appearance of H1N1 influenza virus, initially detected by sentinel systems, was understood as potentially catastrophic in some countries and not in others – and this dramatically affected rates of vaccination as well as levels of trust in public authorities. We might add to these cases the different responses that the detection of radiation after nuclear accidents such as those at Chernobyl and Fukushima has generated in distinctive political and social contexts.

Our approach in this issue is not to condemn the failure of sentinels to incite action; nor, conversely, is it to criticize instances of over-reaction in the absence of definitive threats. Rather, we wish to reflect on the processes through which encroaching potential dangers are made visible, and to ask how the detection of threat can be made to have political force.

A series of problems appears for comparative inquiry. First, there is the question of how a sentinel device is constructed such that a given danger can be perceived: how is a normal background established against which an anomalous signal takes on significance? Can the device distinguish signal from noise? Is it able to detect the unanticipated? Second, we encounter a number of issues around the reliability and legitimacy of sentinel devices: which communities of experts (or non-experts) are authorized to make claims about the meaning of a signal? Does a particular signal travel from center to periphery, or does it take a different route? What interpretive struggles ensue over its implications? And third, we might ask about the challenges of moving from detection to response: how do skeptics cast doubt on the credibility of the sentinel? As a given signal moves across audiences, can the device sustain a sense of collective urgency? And finally, of course, even if there is a collective recognition of the validity of the signal, does it necessarily point to an obvious response?

Sentinel devices have a varied topology, including borders, interfaces, and reservoirs. These devices also entail a variety of modes of transcription, from mapping and modeling to signaling. They combine a diversity of actors, from humans to bears, bees and birds, insofar as they refer to threats common across different species. Finally they allow us to perceive a variety of things, from microscopic entities like toxins, radioactive particles and pathogens to large-scale events like climate change or a pandemic. This issue gathers a range of studies on contemporary sentinels, asking how they make it possible for us to perceive, and possibly to interrupt, the onset of future catastrophe.

A first set of essays focuses on the dynamic relationship between the laboratory and the environment in producing authorized knowledge about health and environmental risks. Sara Wylie shows

"The term *sentinel* has come to describe living beings or technical devices that provide the first signs of an impending catastrophe."

how "citizen science" has made it possible to generate evidence of otherwise invisible hazards—in particular, endocrine disruptors—in local environments. Looking closely at the materiality of the microbiology laboratory, Hannah Landecker examines how experimental animals became accidental sentinels for the epigenetic effects of modern industrial chemicals. Based on her research on malaria control in Dar es Salaam, Ann Kelly describes a technique through which the human body is made into a sentinel for vector populations. And in an historical reflection, Joanna Radin looks at the conjuncture of technical and institutional innovations that made serological epidemiology possible in the 1950s, and at the current uses of old, still-frozen blood samples to yield new knowledge about future risk.

A second group of essays explores public debates around the use of sentinel devices in health policy contexts. Didier Torny and Emmanuel Fillion retrace the French controversy surrounding diethylstilbestrol (DES), one of the first endocrine disruptors to be identified, asking why physicians' warnings about the effects of DES went unheeded. Andrew Lakoff analyzes the controversy that arose over European governments' intensive vaccination campaigns during the 2009 H1N1 influenza pandemic, asking how a relatively weak virus provoked such a strong response. And Emmanuel Didier looks at the use of statistical data by policemen and psychologists, showing how indicators come to link public safety to public health.

Another line of research looks at how animals are made into sentinels for public health. In two essays on avian flu preparedness, scientists see bird populations as a reservoir for human pathogens. Fréderic Keck shows how the city of Hong Kong has been constituted as a sentinel post for pandemic influenza in the wake of the emergence of H5N1 virus in birds. And Lyle Fearnley examines attempts to regulate poultry farming in China, demon-strating how some farms blur the boundary between wild and domesticated birds.

Animals and machines can serve as sentinels for environmental threats that remain invisible to humans. Adriana Petryna looks at how Chernobyl and Fukushima have been taken up as experimental sites to analyze the effects of radiation on animals. Sophie Houdart describes the Large Hadron Collider in Switzerland as a machine designed to capture signals of environmental threat around the globe. And Christelle Gramaglia explores the use of mollusks as sentinel organisms for industrial pollution in a French river system.

How are sentinels produced and interpreted to signal the possible onset of slow-moving catastrophes? In his essay on the bellwether, Jerome Whitington distinguishes among different kinds of sentinels of climate change. Etienne Benson looks at research on polar bears as indicators of snowmelt and species loss in the Arctic. And writing about the famous floating patch of garbage in the Pacific, Baptiste Monsaingeon analyzes the measurement of ocean plastic as an ambivalent indicator of global pollution. In her ethnography of the social practice of wildlife monitoring, Vanessa Manceron describes the world of naturalists in the United Kingdom who regularly survey their "local patch." Chloe Silverman shows how the decline of honeybee populations is measured and turned into a warning signal. Finally, Naomi Oreskes asks why scientists' warnings about climate change have not been taken seriously by the general public, and how the scientific community can more successfully act as a sentinel.

Many of the essays gathered here were initially presented at a colloquium at the Chateau de la Bretesche in Brittany, sponsored by the Borchard Foundation. We are grateful to the Foundation for its generous support of both the colloquium and the production of this issue of LIMN.

FRÉDÉRIC KECK AND **ANDREW LAKOFF**
MAY 2013

limn is published as needed. This issue is set using mostly Christian Schwartz' Graphik and Dino dos Santos' Leitura typefaces. Layout by **Martin Hoyem/American Ethnography**. The General Editors of Limn are **Stephen J. Collier, Christopher M. Kelty,** and **Andrew Lakoff.** Issue No. 3 Editors: **Frédéric Keck and Andrew Lakoff** || This magazine copyright © 2013 Frédéric Keck, Andrew Lakoff and Martin Hoyem. All articles herein are copyright © 2013 by their respective authors. This magazine may not be reproduced without permission, however the articles are available online at http://limn.it/ and available for unrestricted use under a Creative Commons 3.0 unported License, http://creativecommons.org/licenses/by-sa/3.0/ || Publication assistance provided by the Institute for Society and Genetics, University of California, Los Angeles. More at http://limn.it/

The editorial assistant for this issue was **Nick Bartlett,** who is currently a lecturer in Anthropology at USC.

Cover illustration (gouache on paper, 2013) by **Amisha Gadani** showing tumor growth on a barn swallow's beak resulting from radiation in its environment. Amisha lives in Los Angeles and works as the artist in resident in the UCLA evolutionary biology lab of Dr. Michael Alfaro, and in the UCLA Institute for Society and Genetics. Her artwork ranges from paintings and videos to kinetic sculpture and interactive wearables like her on-going series of animal-inspired defensive dresses. Amisha's work has shown in San Francisco, New York, Tokyo, and Pittsburgh and has been featured in Fast Company, Scientific American, and CNet. For more about her work visit her website, www.amishagadani.com

Figures of Warning

THE PROPHET

Prophecy is a classical form in Hebrew religions. Prophets have a vision of the future based on their intimate relationship with God. They are distinguished from other humans by a singular constituency. Spinoza remarks that rather than a specific knowledge, they have a powerful imagination. As their striking images speak to the public, they have often been called demagogues. They communicate with their public not directly but through the mediation of signs, because they aim at reforming human actions rather than transforming the natural world.

 Weber makes a distinction between prophets of fortune and misfortune. This distinction is not only, as Spinoza assumed, a difference between happy and sad individuals, but the result of a collective process of rationalization from one to the other. The first prophets were at the service of kings and would announce the results of war, exalting with their enraged ecstasy the rest of the army. But as Hebrew society became demilitarized, prophets would work for private individuals, giving magical divination, and announcing the collapse of society without being heard. The prophet of misfortune, such as Elias or Jonas, is a lonely figure who can be seen as pathological, but whose visions retrospectively turn out to be true. Prophets are more generally critical figures, facing the king with dreams that mysteriously indicate a discrepancy between the law and the world. Combining affects and language, Hebrew prophecy is a discourse encoded in signs that demands to be deciphered.

THE ORACLE

In classical antiquity, divination took on two distinct forms: that which is inspired by gods (*mantiké,* which comes from *mania, madness*) and that which follows technical rules (*oionostiké*). While Plato saw the second as a form of superstition, Cicero and the Stoïcs, for different reasons, rehabilitated it as a primitive knowledge of nature.

 The Romans put the interpretation of natural phenomena at the heart of their techniques of divination. The observation of the flight of birds (*auspices*), played a significant role in legends of foundation, and was re-enacted for important political decisions—no important decision was taken without consulting the *auguri.* Today, the founding of a public monument is still an "in-auguration." Natural disasters such as epidemics, earthquakes or monstrous births were read by the haruspices as prodigies: signs sent by the gods. Oracles, specialists in the interpretation of signs, were consulted for their omen, or 'true speech'—a truth that would not refer to a present state but to an emerging future

 Divination techniques were the object of philosophical debates raising a tension between science and freedom: is it possible to conceive a natural causality that would include all future events? Would it not contest the principle of contradiction according to which one thing cannot be another at the same time? While Cicero maintained a place for hazard and human freedom, the Stoïcs conceived a world of sympathies or "contagions," in which the relations between beings were revealed by natural events. This conception of the "reason of the world" paved the way for modern medicine.

BIBLIOGRAPHY

Cicero, Marcus Tullius. 2006. *Cicero, On divination, Book 1.* David Wardle, ed. Oxford, U.K.: Oxford University Press.

Koselleck, Reinhardt. 1985. *Futures Past: On the Semantics of Historical Time.* Cambridge, MA.:MIT Press.

THE HERALD

In medieval Europe, heralds are charged with carrying messages to and from the commanders of opposing armies. They are specialists in genealogy: they can trace, on the occasion of tournaments, the history of a family by looking at its arms. This knowledge is called heraldic: the capacity to derive from a visual sign the family blood to which it refers.

Historian Michel Pastoureau has shown that heralds express relations between colors and between animals that are meaningful in medieval societies. The herald is a figure of feudal power: in an unstable society, where alliances are constantly reversed, they traced a minimal order, constituted by feudal relations of descent. At the end of the Middle Ages, they were more and more attached to a noble family, for whom they work as ambassadors. But since they were most often wandering as minstrels, they played a crucial role as arbiters in contested battles for power. In charge of teaching heraldry to sons of kings and knights, they were sometimes also used as alarm clocks.

The herald must therefore be distinguished from the harbinger in the millenarian beliefs of the Middle Ages. While the harbinger announces doom as a divine punishment by the dark mediation of monstrous creatures, the herald makes a clear distinction between friends and foes in an unstable order.

THE PROGNOSTICATOR

The prognosticator is an early modern figure who gathers detailed knowledge of the present in order to reveal how the future is likely to unfold. According to Koselleck, modern secular temporality broke free of the apocalyptic future of Christianity in two movements. First, with the emergence of state-based "rational prognosis" in the late seventeenth century, political strategists wrested control of visions of the future from the Church, distinguishing the temporality of human history from that of nature, and thus bringing the future into the domain of political rationality. For rational prognosis, the future was the product of calculated decisions made in the present, based on a limited number of possibilities: the past contained the elements of what was to come. If this form of future-orientation was thus a "static movement," the next stage—the emergence of a philosophy of progress—opened up an image of the future that transcended the hitherto predictable. The future of this stage was characterized by the increasing speed of its approach and by its unknown quality. An exemplary figure here was the "prophetic philosopher" of the late eighteenth century, whose task was to lead the present toward a future utopia. As Lessing put it, the prophetic philosopher "cannot wait for the future. He wants this future to come more quickly, and he himself wants to accelerate it. "

THE INDICATOR

With the advent of statistics as a technique of government, the indicator constitutes a new mode of relating to the future. As the etymology suggests, the indicator points to a thing without explaining it (in contrast with the measure that seizes a reality). Policies using indicators of economic growth, public health or social inequality do not allow acting on the thing itself but on its trends or movements. An indicator selects from a wide range of information to endorse political action. Governing by indicators means acting on actions without assuming a pre-given order. This form of governing can be characterized as neo-liberal, since it tries to govern at the margins, by using future trends to anticipate actions and yet preserve spontaneity. According to Ted Porter, one of the first occurrences of "indicator" is the description in 1839 of a bird that "indicates to honey hunters where the nests of wild-bees are." Biodiversity is today a conception of nature as an ecosystem in which species are dependent one upon the other. For a bioindicator species, the determining criterion is the number of individuals; for a sentinel organism, what counts is the variation in many parameters at the organic, tissue, cellular or molecular level of each individual. Bioindicators provide a broad overview of the ecological quality of an ecosystem based on the structure and variety of its populations. Sentinel organisms provide more specific data on the noxiousness of pollutants. From qualitative indices of biodiversity or thermodynamics, indicators become quantitative at the end of the 19th century when they point to public health, crime or business. They allow forecasting of a nation's health or the growth based on the observation of some of its elements, such as insanity, height or stock auctions. Indicators are linked to the birth of statistics because the availability of numbers reveals new regularities. But instead of speculating on collective entities, indicators point to a possible action on society – unless, by multiplying indicators, social policy paralyzes action itself.

Pastoureau, Michel. 1979. *Traité d'héraldique.* Paris, Picard Press.

Spinoza, Baruch. 2007. *Theological-Political Treatise.* Jonathan Israel, ed. Cambridge, U.K.: Cambridge University Press.

Weber, Max. 1967. *Ancient Judaism.* Hans Gerth and Don Martindale, eds. New York: Free Press.

The experimental rodent in the polycarbonate cage is the new canary in the coalmine. **Hannah Landecker** explores how environmental signals have slowly started to get clearer and louder.

PHOTO: TATIANA BULYONKOVA

WHEN THE CONTROL BECOMES THE EXPERIMENT

LABORATORY CREATURES AS ACCIDENTAL SENTINELS

Is there such thing as an accidental sentinel, warning of lurking insensible dangers that no one set out to detect? The experimental rodent of twentieth century life science, developed to display nothing but the workings of its inner biology, but becoming instead an accidental indicator of environmental change, might be an instructive example. It was just such a rodent that helped raise the alarm over BPA, now an acronym that floats through the consciousness of the Western consumer today. The story of how BPA or bisphenol-A, an organic compound used to make certain plastics that is also an endocrine disruptor that mimics the action of estrogen in the body, came

to the attention of the plastic-bottle-sipping public has been detailed in a number of places. In most accounts, the chemical compounds or the scientist-investigators who study its health effects are the main characters (Vogel 2012). Here the story is retold with a focus on the control animal – in this case a laboratory mouse.

The story goes as follows: In 1998, biologist Patricia Hunt was studying the biology of infertility by using mouse strains that have unusually high numbers of chromosomal abnormalities resulting from aberrant meiosis. Meiosis is the kind of cell division that leads to germ cells – to sperm cells in male organisms and egg cells in females. Hunt's research was mo-

tivated by problems of human reproduction; the wrong number of chromosomes in eggs - aneuploidy—is a leading cause of miscarriage, congenital birth defects and mental retardation in humans. As is standard in experiments, Hunt also used "control" animals, supposedly normal mice, as a comparison - such animals are often referred to as "wild-type" if they do not carry the mutant genotype being tested although there is nothing wild about them. Hunt's control animals went through all the same interventions and experiences as the mutants used to study the chromosomal abnormalities.

The main function of the control animal is to pick up biological outcomes that might result from extraneous elements of the experimental protocol, rather than arising from the experimental intervention being tested or the mutation under study in the experimental animal. One week, out of the blue, Hunt found, "the control numbers were just completely bonkers" in more than one of her experiments; about 40% of the normal female mice suddenly began to suffer from failures of chromosomal alignment during meiosis (quoted in Gross 2007; see also Hunt et al. 2003). Upon a systematic review of the handling of the mice over the previous weeks, Hunt and her coworkers determined that the plastic cages in which the animals lived, and their water bottles, had been washed using a high pH detergent and sterilized at high heat. This caused the polycarbonate plastic to leach small amounts of chemicals, including bisphenol-A, which the animals ingested in their drinking water and absorbed through their skin.

Testing BPA by itself, Hunt then determined that the substance could be used to intentionally induce higher rates of these chromosomal abnormalities in the eggs of normal mice—compared of course to non-BPA-exposed controls (Hunt et al. 2003, 2009). In this way, the control subject of one experiment became the test animal in the next. Further research has raised the question of whether there is any such a thing as a non-BPA-exposed organism today: A recent review of the literature on BPA's potential role in obesity concludes that, "all human fetuses that have been examined have measurable blood levels of BPA, and mean or median levels found in humans are higher than levels found in fetal and neonatal mice in response to maternal doses that increase postnatal growth" (vom Saal et al. 2012).

Laboratory organisms began living in plastic instead of glass or metal enclosures about the same time Western consumer society was also making the switch in the middle of the twentieth century. However, awareness that something in the plastic could have negative effects on reproduction and health emerged much later, and was made possible in part by laboratory accidents such as Hunt's starting in the 1990s. In another lab, estrogen-sensitive cancer cells cultured in plastic dishes suddenly began to act as though they were being dosed with estrogen after a biological supply company changed the plastic composition of the bottles storing the nutrient medium used to culture the cells. Biologist Ana Soto and her collaborators determined that the substance feeding the cells' estrogen-mediated response was nonylphenol, another endocrine-disrupting estrogen mimic used in making polymers and detergents (Vandenberg et al. 2010).

The general category of "endocrine-disruptor" emerged as an issue of concern and debate during the 1990s. The book *Our Stolen Future* called attention to the effects of hormone mimics in industrial and waste effluent on wildlife, showing how the resulting abnormalities of sex development and reproductive damage were threatening exposed fish, amphibian and bird populations (Colborn et al. 1996). This context made it more likely that experimenters such as Hunt and Soto would be attuned to vacillations of the control numbers caused by industrially-derived substances. In addition, the larger

research interest in endocrine disruptors gave them a body of science to contribute to when the control animal exited the periphery of the experiment and became the finding.

The story that has unfolded from here is one in which the effects of endocrine disruptors such as BPA are tested directly, at "environmentally-relevant" levels – that is, the kind of exposures humans living with plastics in contemporary industrialized societies might experience—on animals, particularly as they develop *in utero*. The findings have been racking up: Female mice and rats exposed to low doses prenatally grow into adults that suffer breast cancers and reproductive abnormalities at higher rates than unexposed animals; BPA easily crosses the placenta in humans and other animals, and affects placental cells themselves in terms of gene expression; BPA causes epigenetic changes in developing tissues that in turn shift patterns of gene expression potential in the adult animals, causing changes such as increased adiposity (Vandenberg et al. 2009; vom Saal et al. 2012).

These findings remain contested in terms of their translation into regulatory action, in part because chemical toxicity testing traditionally has not looked at low dose effects in developing organisms, but at high dose toxicity in adults. In other words, looking for long-term disturbances to reproductive biology due to low exposures during development is a very different test than looking for cancers, poisoning, or heart attacks in adult animals exposed to high amounts of a substance. However, the rapidly expanding field of environmental epigenetics has underscored the legitimacy of such a lifespan perspective. It provides both a logic and a technical means for measuring environmental harm that lodges in the body—not as a lesion, mutation in DNA, or a toxic effect immediately visible as a birth defect or a poisoning—but rather as a shift in gene regulation and gene expression with important long-term, rather than short-term, health effects. Environmental epigenetics, with its focus on the setting or re-setting of the molecules controlling gene expression in cells, provides a powerful framework for transforming environmental harm into epigenetic harm (Landecker 2011).

What is the role of the experimental animal, and in particular the control experimental animal as an accidental sentinel, in physically registering the envi-

ronmentally-relevant dose and making visible epigenetic harm? The control animal is a check or comparison, and appears in experimentation because "a discoverable fact is a difference or a relation, and a discovered datum has significance only as it is related to a frame of reference, to a relatum" (Boring 1954). The relatum—the control—is injected with saline solution where the test animal gets the real deal; the control animal is cut open even if no surgical change is then effected, while the test animal has something ablated or manipulated. It is fed the same things, handled the same way, and housed in the same conditions as the test animal. It experiences the experiment, but is supposed to weather it all and remain that against which the experimental intervention may be measured. It is the ground against which difference may be achieved; it is supposed to keep the experiment honest.

In the attention to control numbers that "go bonkers," the frame of reference comes to the fore, instead of receding into the background of necessary but banal experimental procedure. The control reveals "environment" where there is presumed to be none of consequence. The experimental rodent in a polycarbonate cage eating chow pellets accidentally revealed material harm in the environment in the very place the "environment" is most suppressed. The environment of environmentalism – rivers and lakes, air and earth and trees – could not be further from these experimental spaces built on the premise of control. No one set out to look for these warning signs of impending environmental danger, in fact, no one thought to look for these particular environmental harms, in part because the cage, the water bottle, the culture medium, the food, were the background to the organismal biology in the foreground and had no presence as "the environment"—until these abnormalities were evident.

This story may look like one of contingency, out of which many scientific discoveries have arisen. Just think penicillin, and Pasteur's declaration that "chance favors the prepared mind." But look one level deeper: The rodent in the polycarbonate cage shows the contingency in this story to be fundamentally structured by human industrial activity. The "accident" of the accidental sentinel is not that of fate or chance, but one of attention. Thanks both to the widespread use of the model organism in biological science in the twentieth century and the ensuing interest of historians of science in the role of model organisms in generating twentieth century life science, we know a great deal about the production of experimental rodents in terms of their selection, genetic manipulation, and breeding (Rader 2004). We know next-to-nothing – because we have thought next-to-nothing – about how they have been fed and housed.

The production of mice with certain gene knockouts or transgenic additions was and still is central to many areas of genetic research. The intense refinement of experimental rodents as an instrument of genetics – an attempt to purify them by holding everything still while just changing one component of the animals' genome – has paradoxically brought the background of such experiments into view. And what we see there is this: While these animals might have been bred to be model organisms of particular human diseases or ailments – such as infertility – they or their "wild-type" counterparts raised under identical conditions have become unintentional models of the sedentary "ad libitum," plastic-infused, nutritionally synthetic lives of contemporary North American human animals.

Experimental animals share, to a greater extent than is normally recognized, the habitat of their keepers – and this goes for much more than the plastic water bottles. Consider the finding that the control rodents kept under standard laboratory protocol used in biomedical research and preclinical drug testing in the United States are metabolically morbid: "Compared to those that are fed less, exercise more, and have a stimulating environment, animals maintained under the standard laboratory conditions are relatively overweight, insulin resistant, hypertensive, and are likely to experience premature death" (Martin et al. 2010). Elsewhere, attempts to test the effects of certain micronutrients or endocrine disruptors on developing or newborn mice have accidentally focused attention on the biological effects of standard synthetic or "natural" experimental animal diets (Waterland et al. 2006). Extensive interest in the role of "environmental enrichment" in affecting brain development and the making of new neurons in adults has brought attention to the "standard" environment of the control to which an "enriched" environment must be compared. Enrichment begs the question: Enriched compared to what? What lasting effects on the biology and behavior of generations of standard control rodents have resulted from living in a few square feet of bedding covered cage with continuous access to an overhead dispenser full of dry pellet food and no exercise wheel? Against what condition, what relatum, does one measure enrichment and its neurological effects?

It is impossible to say how many experiments have simply been discarded, discontinued, or judged to have "failed" when controls went awry, rather than interpreted as problems that signal some-thing fundamentally wrong in the cage environment. For the control animal to have become an accidental sentinel, someone had to interpret the indication of danger, to see it as meaningful, and invert the experiment, bringing the control into the role of test subject in its own right. It is overreaching to conclude that control animals have somehow in themselves *caused* the reading and registering of environmentally relevant exposures and their potential epigenetic harms. However, as biomedical research looks increasingly to experimentally trace the developmental and epigenetic effects of environmental exposures, from nutrition to stress to pollution to exercise to visual stimulation, the standard cage environment of the twentieth century experimental rodent, which shares so much with the environment of the twentieth century industrialized human, is increasingly beginning to register as a measure and probe of environmental harm. If the canary in the coal mine was the warning figure for an age of the extraction of raw materials and the onset of industrialization, the experimental rodent in the polycarbonate cage may be seen as the warning figure for the early twenty-first century and the legacies of industrialization. ▪

HANNAH LANDECKER *teaches in the Department of Sociology and the Institute for Society and Genetics at UCLA.*

REFERENCES

Boring, Edwin G. 1954. "The Nature and History of Experimental Control." *The American Journal of Psychology,* 67(4):573–589.

Colborn, Theo, Dianne Dumanoski, and John Peterson Myers. 1996. *Our Stolen Future: Are We Threatening Our Fertility, Intelligence, and Survival?* New York: Dutton.

Gross, Lisa. 2007. "The Toxic Origins of Disease." *PLoS Biol,* 5(7):e193. doi:10.1371/journal.pbio.0050193.

Hadlow, W.J., Edward Grimes, and George Jay Jr. 1955. "Stilbestrol Contaminated Feed and Reproductive Disturbances in Mice." *Science* 122(3171):643–644.

Hunt, Patricia, Martha Susiarjo, Carmen Rubio, and Terry Hassold. 2009. "The Bisphenol A Experience: A Primer for the Analysis of Environmental Effects on Mammalian Reproduction." *Biology of Reproduction,* 81: 807–813.

Hunt, Patricia, Kara Koehler, Martha Susiarjo, Craig Hodges, Arlene Ilagan, Robert Voigt, Sally Thomas, Brian Thomas, and Terry Hassold. 2003. "Bisphenol A Exposure Causes Meiotic Aneuploidy in the Female Mouse." *Current Biology,* 13(7):546–553.

Landecker, Hannah. 2011. "Food as Exposure: Nutritional Epigenetics and the New Metabolism." *BioSocieties,* 6:167–194.

Martin, Bronwen, Sunggoan Ji, Stuart Maudsley, and Mark Mattson. 2010. "'Control' laboratory rodents are metabolically morbid: Why it matters." *PNAS* 107(14):6127–6133.

Rader, Karen. 2004. *Making Mice: Standardizing Animals for American Biomedical Research.* Princeton: Princeton University Press.

Vandenberg, Laura, Maricel Maffini, Carlos Sonnenschein, Beverly Rubin, and Ana Soto.2010. "Bisphenol-A and the Great Divide: A Review of Controversies in the Field of Endocrine Disruption." *Endocrine Reviews* 30(1):75–95.

Vogel, Sarah.2012. *Is It Safe? BPA and the Struggle to Define the Safety of Chemicals.* Berkeley: California University Press.

vom Saal, Frederick, Susan Nagel, Benjamin Coe, Brittany Angle, and Julia Taylor. 2012. "The estrogenic endocrine disrupting chemical bisphenol A (BPA) and obesity." *Molecular and Cellular Endocrinology,* 354:74-84.

Waterland, Robert, Juan-Ru Lin, Charlotte Smith, and Randy Jirtle. 2006. "Post-weaning Diet Affects Genomic Imprinting at Insulin-like Growth Factor 2 (Igf2) Locus." *Human Molecular Genetics,* 15(5):705–716.

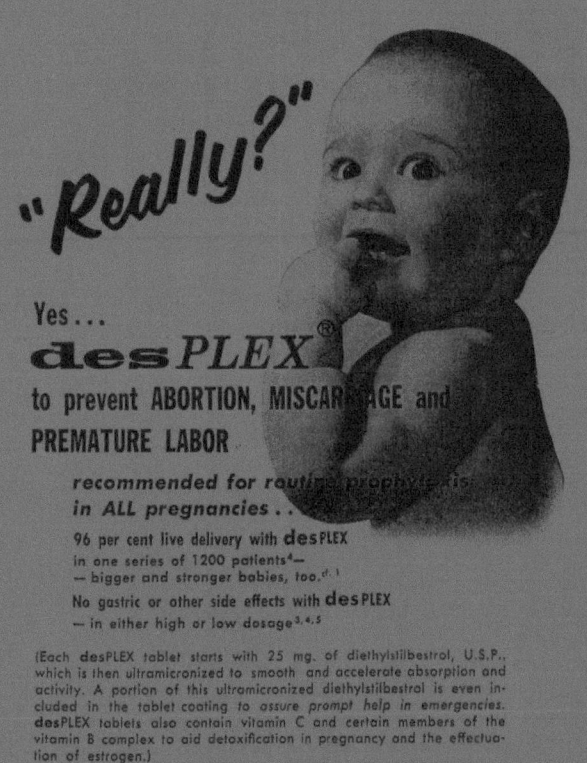
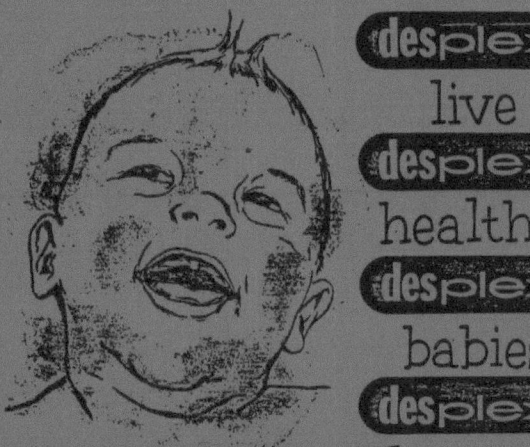
MECHANISMS OF INVISIBILITY

FORGOTTEN SENTINELS OF DIETHYLSBESTROL PROGENY

DIETHYLSTILBESTROL WAS ONE OF THE FIRST IDENTIFIED ENDOCRINE DISRUPTORS. HOWEVER, EFFORTS TO WARN FRENCH PHYSICIANS ABOUT THE DRUG'S POTENTIALLY DANGEROUS EFFECTS ON PREGNANT WOMEN FAILED. **EMMANUELLE FILLON** AND **DIDIER TORNY** SHOW HOW SENTINELS SOMETIMES DON'T WORK. ➲

"The effects seen in in utero DES*-exposed humans parallel those found in contaminated wildlife and laboratory animals, suggesting that humans may be at risk to the same environmental hazards as wildlife."*

Wingspread Declaration, 1991

IN APRIL 1970, Arthur Herbst and Robert Scully reported in *Cancer* the identification of six definitive cases of cell vaginal cancer in girls and young women all between 15 and 22 years old. Continuing the investigation through a case-control study, the Herbst team published its findings in the *New England Journal of Medicine:*

This form of cancer was significantly associated with diethylstilbestrol (DES) use by the patients' mothers during the first trimester of pregnancy. DES, a hormone synthesized by Doods in 1938 in England and approved by the FDA in 1941, had been widely prescribed by physicians to prevent miscarriages throughout the developed world in the following decades. Their study on DES effects was the first time a link was shown between taking a medicine during pregnancy and a subsequent morbid effect with considerable temporal distance on the offspring.

Since the early 1970s, the list of actual or potential effects of *in utero* DES exposure has grown steadily to include infertility, high prematurity, urogenital malformations, cancers, psychiatric disorders, eating disorders, congenital oesophagial stenosis, and other conditions. Populations found to be affected by exposure started with "DES daughters" but were later found to also include "DES sons" and "DES grandchildren." A new category of disease thus appeared: transgenerational diseases.

In 1991, a group of scientists met at the initiative of Theo Colborn and Pete Myers, American researchers searching for links between environmental exposures and health. All of them were concerned about the effects of chemicals as a potential threat to reproduction of enormous scope. They stated that DES was the first endocrine disruptor identified. Accordingly, the lessons relating to DES should provide the necessary model to anticipate threats posed by other substances to animal and human development. However, the previous history of this molecule shows a complete lack of precaution about its side effects.

The disregard of repeated warnings marked the US history of regulating DES from the first prescriptions in the 1940s until physicians were ordered to stop prescribing the drug to pregnant women in 1971 (Langston 2009). The French story goes beyond what happened in the USA: DES prescription began in the early 1950s and peaked in the late 1960s; it was recommended for use in pregnant women until 1976 and—unlike the case in the USA—continued to be used marginally until at least 1982. Our work on French DES raises the question of why scientific warnings about the dangerous effects of the drug did not have a "sentinel" effect. In the following pages, we will show different mechanisms of invisibility that prevented public knowledge and collective learning.

Considering pharmacovigilance about side effects of DES as a drug, we observe the repeated tragedy of institutional neglect leading to long-term health problems among DES progeny. Looking at DES with environmentalist glasses as a precursor substance of endocrine disruptors (ED), we see a wide mobilization and a pro-active vigilance: the studies of DES exposure along with observations of wildlife in polluted environments shaped the Wingspread Declaration in 1991 (Krimsky 2000). And twenty years after the declaration, DES is used routinely in animal experiments to measure the effects of other suspected endocrine disruptors.

In short, the DES story is that of a disastrous medical and social experiment that was later identified as having created valuable precedents helping to trigger the development of new tools to prevent similar damage (Chateauraynaud & Torny 2005). These two successive movements are typical "late lessons from early warnings" in which collective learning took place slowly in the USA, and even more so in France.

In North America, after the initial harms of DES were shown, the medical establishment in the 1970s quickly mobilized to mitigate damages and subsequently established follow-up cohorts to monitor health problems in DES offspring. DES victims mobilized later in the French case, and more than two decades separate the American and French DES tort law trials. The French history can therefore shed a different light on the legacy of DES: It poses the question of how knowledge about transgenerational diseases was not built on these sentinel populations. In other words, under what circumstances does an alert not lead to action?

A NON-EXISTENT SENTINEL GROUP: DES-EXPOSED PROGENY

Understanding the non-existence of sentinel populations in the DES case first requires exploring prescription patterns in the 1950s and 1960s in France. In the absence of standardized guidelines and without any pharmacovigilance infrastructure, prescription requirements were highly variable. Herbst's 1971 discovery was not widely disseminated in France because of weak links between French obstetricians and the American epidemiological universe. When Herbst spoke at a conference in Paris in 1972, most obstetrician-gynecologists did not believe in the risk of cancer caused by DES for their patients. The doubts of this audience were in part due to differences in principle—the hormonal theory of miscarriages still masked the genetic theory—and, more pragmatically, due to the claim made by many French doctors that DES was prescribed in far lower doses in their country. Only a handful of clinicians "recalled" their patients so they could inform their daughters. Most notable among this group was Dr. Jeanine Henry-Suchet, who attempted to mobilize her colleagues to act, but did not succeed. As a result, in the 1970s, most girls exposed *in utero* were unaware of their exposure and its attendant risks. Even when the contraindication of DES for pregnant women was adopted in 1977, there were no traces of a public discussion.

Worried by new results concerning fertility problems suffered by "DES daughters" and by some uterine malformations in her patients, Dr. Anne Cabau searched for DES daughters through the magazine of a mutual benefit society in 1981 and published some clinical results. Following Cabau's piece, *le Monde* published an article titled "A Monumental Mistake" in 1983, which was widely quoted by mainstream media. Most public health institutions took reassuring stances, stating that the problem was already widely known and mostly a matter of the past. A group of scientists mobilized by the "French NIH" (INSERM) issued recommendations outlining how to support and inform patients. But these recommendations remained a dead letter despite the scientists' conclusion that 160,000 children had been exposed *in utero* to the drug.

In 1988, following the advocacy of a patient's association, a group of clinicians and researchers met at the Ministry of Health to develop a brochure about the dangers of DES. The vast majority of these experts rejected distributing the brochure to patients, arguing it should only target health care professionals. As a result of doctors' resistance to broader outreach and education, the effect of this initial campaign was very limited. A second campaign was launched in 1992, and in 2003 AFSSAPS, the "French FDA" did it again. But the level of knowledge among gynecologists stayed very low as they felt they were not concerned.

Even today, some clinicians claim they have "never met a DES daughter" whilst some women displayed many symptoms (ectopic pregnancies, late miscarriages, etc.) for years without having their condition correctly diagnosed. Researching and disseminating information about the history and effects of DES was largely left to the doctors and the unspecialized media who were willing to cover the issue. As a result, misdiagnosis and inappropriate care, sometimes iatrogenic, were—if not the rule—at least a very common experience for these women.

USELESS SENTINELS OR HOW TO AVOID PUBLICIZING DES KNOWLEDGE

Three distinct mechanisms kept DES knowledge limited in the French case: the failure to build sound epidemiological cohorts, the lack of visibility of "dedicated" clinical structures, and finally the very weak dissemination of epidemiological and clinical knowledge.

Today, the absence of a tracked cohort of exposed population in France is striking. Indeed, to date, authorities have not even attempted to build a vaginal cancer registry. While the information campaign of 1992 supported by DES Action International was presented in France as a "screening" campaign, it did not lead to anything lasting, unlike in the Netherlands where large cohorts of exposed research subjects were built around the same time. Today, in France, the only ongoing research on DES is two small clinical surveillance follow-up studies that do not collect epidemiological data. Consequently, French doctors must rely on Dutch and American cohorts for information related to the effects of DES exposure on the third generation and psychological effects or cancer prevalence in mature women of the second generation. Moreover, the knowledge derived from all these cohorts remained relatively confined.

Indeed, the limited clinical knowledge that has been gathered to date remains in the hands of a small number of people. Info-DES, an association mainly composed of DES mothers, in the early 1990s worked with mobilized clinicians to build the first French forums offering information and clinical follow-up to affected patients. But these consultations have never been labeled as such by public authorities or even by lodging hospitals. As a result, DES patients generally must already know their status and proactively contact an association to obtain medical social or legal support.

The very few DES consultations that have taken place since the 1990s allowed for experimentation and adaptation techniques (such as relocation of a sole embryo in AMP, specific suture techniques to avoid late miscarriages, etc.) that were never publicized. Information flowed between associations and the limited number clinicians who saw first-hand the effects of DES, but the limited number of scientific publications published on the topic gained little interest. It was only intervention by the Réseau-DES, which followed up on Info-DES, that the circulation of knowledge was organized: in the late 1990s, this small association established a scientific advisory board that reviewed various controversial issues and mobilized official health agencies on specific topics. Réseau-DES was also responsible for the release of the first patient-focused brochure in 2008.

France's policy concerning maternity leave for DES daughters illustrates ongoing problems plaguing the national response to DES. Drawing on long-documented medical studies showing that the best prevention of late miscarriages is full rest for pregnant women, Réseau-DES lobbied and advocated for maternity leave for DES daughters for more than fifteen years. Their efforts were unsuccessful until 2010, a time when most DES daughters were nearing the end of their reproductive lives. Moreover, in practice, doctors and social security administrators today still rarely know about this recently adopted policy. An invisibility mechanism is thus replicated from mother to daughter, and extended from the medical field to social life.

A SINGULAR HISTORY OR HOW ENDOCRINE DISRUPTORS DID NOT TRANSFORM DES

If DES is perpetually forgotten and neglected, it is in part because it initially appeared as a peculiar story. Health problems associated with DES have been for many years minimized as they were documented, rarely subjected to systematic collection, and rarely linked to broader public health issues such as drug pharmacovigilance or transgenerational exposure. This singularization work that has characterized the French response to DES began with those that bear the greatest public health concern and responsibility for launching alerts. Dr. Henry-Suchet's research on very young French DES daughters showed changes in vaginal cellular structures that were not present in those exposed to ethinyl-estradiol. As a result, hormonal treatments in general were not questioned except in relation to this one drug. At the same moment when the first case of vaginal cancer appeared in 1975, French pharmacovigilance was founded on the basis of anti-poisoning centers and was therefore focused on short-term effects of substances, unlike the US epidemiological model, which was able to trace long-term effects. In this context, when some DES effects were finally taken seriously in 1977, it remained the only drug known with long-term demonstrated effects.

Associative work went in the same direction: It was primarily focused on information related to providing clinical care for DES daughters until 2000. Debates about oral contraception or the controversy over hormone replacement therapy which received major attention worldwide had no echo in this little DES world. The creation of an association focused on parenting, Filles-DES, reinforced this trend: ovarian stimulation to get pregnant through AMP, for example, was not seen as problematic. It was only when another association, Hhorages, was created in 2002 that a shift in framing—from "DES drug" to "DES substance"—occurred. For the first time, DES was not seen as an isolated case, but was included among the various artificial hormones given to pregnant women and, therefore, to which their fetuses are exposed. Centered on the recognition of psychological effects of DES exposure, this association is run by parents whose DES-exposed progeny experienced serious psychological problems, often resulting in suicide. They blame all hormonal treatments, and thus attempt to expand the range of acknowledged deleterious effects in DES offspring to include other widely prescribed hormones. Hhorages collects data from its members and seek alliances, especially among toxicologists and endocrinologists specializing in environmental issues who often occupy the position of snipers within their own discipline. One of the most visible results of this collaboration is a co-authored article published in *Fertility & Sterility* in 2011 describing the increase of hypospadias, the defect of the urethra in males that involves an abnormally placed urinary meatus, a condition typically labeled an ED effect, among DES grandsons. Nevertheless, this transformation in the ED paradigm was not embraced by some French DES associations, which criticized that publication as "sensationalist." At the heart of this debate lies the question of transmissibility: Did the nightmare stop with DES daughters or should exposure to the hormone be viewed as a real transgenerational threat for these daughters' own progeny? ■

EMMANUELLE FILLION *is a health and disability sociologist. She works on sanitary crises, medical affairs and the legal mobilizations of patients and persons with disabilities.* **DIDIER TORNY** *is a senior researcher in sociology, whose work examines private and public normative action relating to health.*

REFERENCES

Chateauraynaud, Francis, and Didier Torny. 2005. "Mobilising around a risk: From alarm raisers to alarm carriers." in *Risques et crises alimentaires*, ed. Cecile Lahellec, pp. 329-339. Paris: Lavoisier. (http://halshs.archives-ouvertes.fr/docs/00/41/18/47/PDF/Alarmcarriers.pdf)

Krimsky, Sheldon. 2000. *Hormonal chaos: The scientific and social origins of the environmental endocrine hypothesis*. Baltimore: Johns Hopkins University Press.

Langston, Nancy. 2009. *Toxic bodies: Hormone disruptors and the legacy of DES*. New Haven and London: Yale University Press.

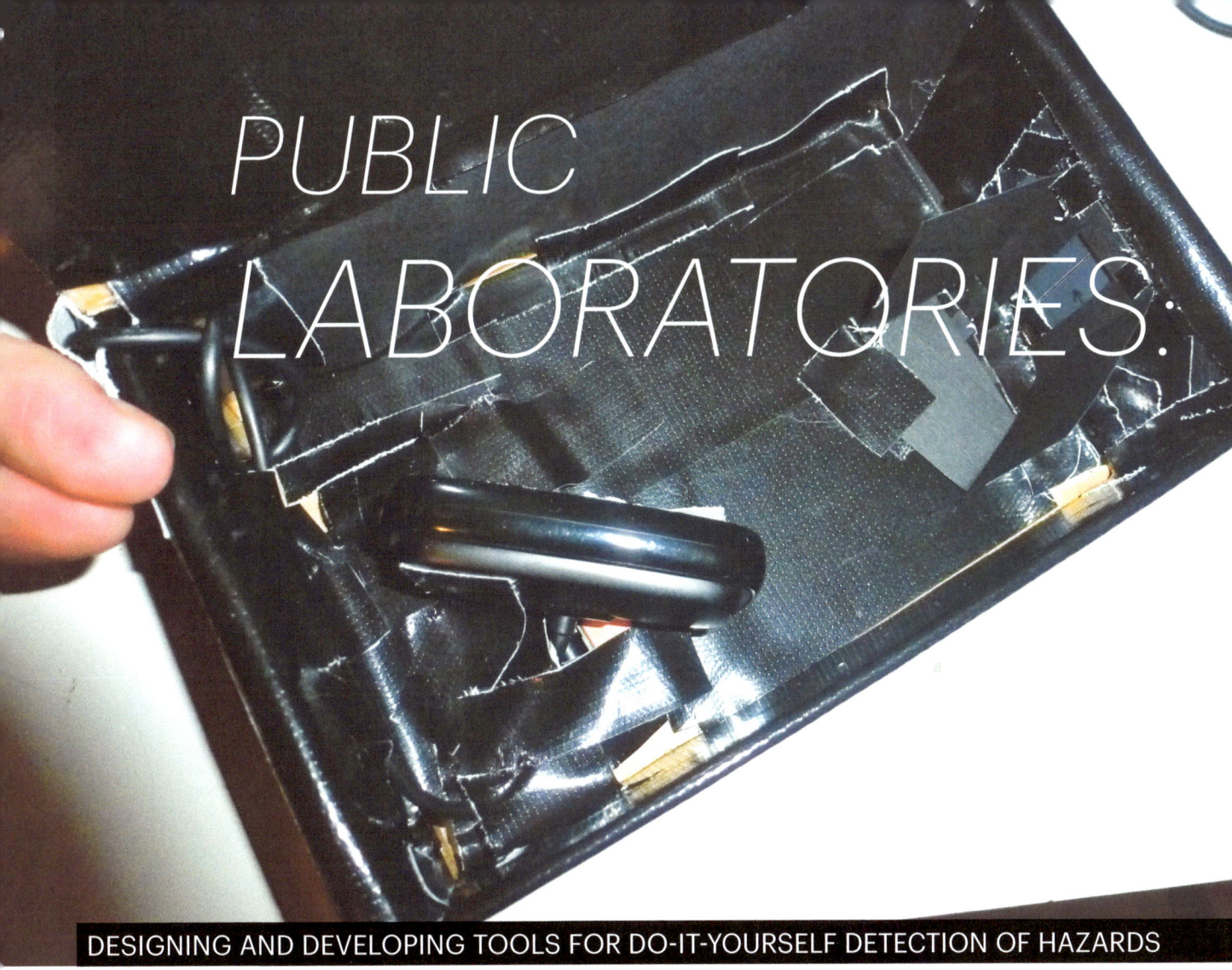

PUBLIC LABORATORIES:

Signals of environmental hazard cannot be heard unless there is a device to detect them. **Sara Wylie, Megan McLaughlin** and **Josh McIlvain** show you how to make one yourself.

INDUSTRIALIZATION HAS CHANGED THE VERY BIOCHEMISTRY OF the planet. Daily our bodies are exposed to a range of perceptible and imperceptible hazards. Everyday products are comprised of a laundry list of unrecognizable chemicals. Any given human's body fat, blood and tissues bear a similar list of chemicals, an inscribed history of his or her contact with the environment. Consumers cannot adequately analyze and assess potential threats posed by the accumulation and activity of these chemicals in their bodies. Environmental Health sciences have not caught up with the realities of ubiquitous, complex and interactive chemical exposures. Scientists and regulators are struggling to conceptualize and study how health end points like obesity, cancers, infertility and ADHD are linked to gene-environment interactions that begin from the moment of conception and depend upon an individual's unique genetic and life history. Corporate and industrial actors spreading misinformation and doubt confound the biological and social investigation of industrial hazards and make environmental health threats harder to study. As we know from work in science studies, laboratory tools are ill equipped to study the expanse of environmental health questions, even as they are being answered by our bodies, other organisms and our environments. How can exposed individuals learn to see these changes, how can a non-professional

PUBLIC LABORATORIES

public become involved in generating knowledge about their environmental conditions? How might we build not only DIY sentinel devices but also a new public grassroots infrastructure for the discovery and analysis of pressing environmental health issues?

Public Laboratory, a non-profit dedicated to the open source development of DIY tools for environmental investigation, believes we must become investigators of our own environments. They turn the detritus of contemporary living—VHS boxes, broken CD's, old film canisters—into tools to identify and study the hazards around us. Their low cost test for Hydrogen Sulfide (H_2S), a neurotoxic byproduct of gas extraction, involves putting photographic paper into classic black film canisters (Horwell et al. 2004, Horwell et al. 2005). Public Lab's spectrometer is comprised of a broken CD, black VHS box and cheap webcam. A slit in the side of the VHS box enables light from the specimen to enter the box. This light, refracted into a rainbow by the CD's diffraction gradient, is then recorded by a webcam placed in the top of the VHS box. Public Lab members, people who sign up online to participate in the community's open source hardware and software development, investigate whether it can be used to identify chemicals and hazards in everyday products:

Three years ago I graduated from Kansas State University with an undergraduate degree in general physics, got married, left home to be a Christian missionary, and I didn't look back. I did not (and still don't) intend to use my training in physics professionally, but I do consider science to be an important part of life that many students and even adults shy away from, because so many scientists have made the field seem untouchable to "ordinary" people. I originally came across the Public Lab project when searching for plans to make a spectrometer, as a way to measure the color temperature of a light source. What I found at Public Lab was not just instructions for a home-made spectrometer, but a group of people with a similar desire as myself: to make science accessible, understandable, and affordable for ordinary people.

While a spectrometer can be used for so many different purposes, one of the most well-known is to determine the composition substance by the way light interacts with it. Not only can a spectrometer help to identify a substance by looking at what light

is emitted from it, but also by looking at what light it absorbs. I used my home-made spectrometer to do both of these in an experiment using ultraviolet light fluorescence. For many substances, UV light has enough energy that the substance will absorb it, then emit some extra energy in the form of a lower energy photon.

In my experiment, I used ultraviolet light to check several liquids for fluorescence. While many different substances will fluoresce under UV light, I was looking for a certain dye used by many laundry detergents. Most detergents use this fluorescent dye to make your clothes look brighter and whiter, because it will actually glow when hit with sunlight (which contains UV). However, my wife and I use cloth diapers for our two children, and this dye has the tendency to build up in cloth and not wash out, which decreases the absorbency of the cloth (not good at all for cloth diapers). Many detergents claim to be "free and clear" or something similar, but still contain this dye.[1] To check these claims, I shone UV light on detergent samples, and compared the resulting spectra to a baseline UV spectrum. Those detergents using the dye absorbed light from the UV area of the spectrum, and re-emitted it in lower-energy areas, usually around blue or cyan. Those that showed little change from the baseline UV spectrum do not use the dye. Using this process, we chose to use a detergent that did not use this dye. This is how the home-made spectrometer was useful for us, and I look forward to more ways that science can be made useful in the lives of "ordinary" people. (Josh McIlvain, Public Lab Member, September 2012.)

---

1   The fluorescent properties of brighteners has also been used by Seventh Generation, an ecologically friendly detergent company, as part of a social media campaign to encourage people to discover for themselves reasons for switching brands. This campaign asked people to submit images of clothes glowing under black light due to brighteners (Newman 2010). Josh's DIY spectrometry case differs in providing data in an authoritative format, the spectra, which might conceivably be used to identify exactly what chemical brightener is being used in this "free and clear" product.

◂ **PREVIOUS PAGE AND LEFT:** Josh's home spectrometry set up. This page shows spectrometer (left), sample (baby food jar) and light source (UV flashlight). For more info on the setup, see Public Lab research note:
http://publiclaboratory.org/notes/joshmc/4-28-2012/setup-uv-testing-specrtrometer

Laboratory spectrometers can cost thousands of dollars, but the components required to make a basic one are inexpensive and commonly available. When he searched through the spectrometry tool page on Public Lab's website, Josh found video instructionals, written explanations, photo documentation and a parts list that enabled him to build his own spectrometer. He also joined the active listserv to find out about what others working on the spectrometry tool were doing. Through Public Lab's website, an evolving framework for collaborative open source hardware development, Josh could become part of community building this tool and share the results of his work. The spectra he recorded were uploaded to Public Lab through open source free software—Spectral Workbench. This software allowed Josh to share, align and analyze his spectra with other members. By enabling new approaches such as open hardware development for developing environmental health research tools, Public Lab acts as an infrastructure for DIY sentinel devices.

After Josh successfully built his spectrometer with help from the online community at Public Lab, he began to participate in activities known among Public Lab's members as "Civic Technoscience". Performed by individual members of the public to investigate questions of importance to their daily life (Fortun and Fortun 2005), Civic Technoscience is a mode of science that enables people to become credible generators of new knowledge about their environments and conditions using tools they can understand, build and adapt themselves (Wylie *et. al* forthcoming). For Josh, this meant he became a contributor by submitting "research notes" on wiki-pages describing his experiences assembling spectrometers and detailing his findings. His research is a kind of "hello world experiment" that shows the spectrometer might support new forms of consumer activism and environmental investigation of hazards that have traditionally have been hard to see and study.

Brighteners are in many ways a quintessential example of such an imperceptible hazard: a product of industrial chemistry, this ubiquitous consumer good gives clothes the appearance of cleanliness by coating them in chemicals. While Josh became interested in brighteners because he noticed they reduced water absorbency in his child's diapers, others, also drawing on personal experiences, have expressed concerns about their potential harm as allergens.[2] Research from the 1970s indicates that optical brighteners can cause contact dermatitis—including rashes and irritation—when mixing with sweat and absorbing into skin (Osmundsen 1969, Osmundsen and Alani 1971). However, more recent scientific studies con-

test those findings (Belsito 2002). Consumers, through the work of concerned individuals like Josh, operating homemade tools such as the spectrometer and Public Lab, could collectively investigate and archive claims that detergents are "free and clear" and potentially the elucidate links between brighteners and dermatitis at a grassroots level. Public Lab is working towards building a public archive containing spectra from thousands of such individual investigations into the contents of common household and enable collective civic inquiries to identify and campaign against a range of unsafe consumer products.[3] To this end, Public Lab launched the Spectral Challenge in March 2013, a crowdfunded, public competition to improve the process for open source spectrometry and develop real-world use cases like Josh's.[4]

How might individual investigations be connected to new forms of environmental health advocacy aiming to reshape industrial infrastructures? A second Public Lab project investigates how civic technoscience might document and help mobilize action against a by-product associated with natural gas extraction-Hydrogen Sulfide (H_2S). In September of 2011, Public Laboratory members met with residents of Garfield County, Colorado who had recently organized to sample one family's indoor air quality because of the smells coming from their tap water. Analysis of the sample showed H_2S levels of more than 185 times above EPA's recommended long-term exposure level. The family, in which the son developed painful skin lesions coincident with this exposure, was forced to abandon their home. Neighboring gas development companies denied that nearby natural gas extraction operations were connected to the water contamination (Colson 2011, GCM 2011). The environmental health manager for the county responded to these reports by saying that the neighboring gas wells had been "closed in" and could not be the source of the H_2S (Colson 2011).

H_2S, which smells like rotten eggs, can readily be detected by humans at very low concentrations. But as the case above shows, concerned people can struggle to determine the source of H_2S contamination. To help communities who smell H_2S map the source, Public Lab is adapting a method developed by a volcanologist who studies the sources of the smelly gas (Horwell 2004,et al., Horwell et al. 2005). Their method uses photographic paper which tarnishes (turning brown after oxidizing) when its silver halide (the photo responsive element) is exposed to H_2S. Compared to commercial meters that cost a few hundred dollars and are difficult for non-professionals to use, the test Public Lab is developing, utilizing film canisters that prevent light exposure but allow air circulation, only costs a few cents a test and can easily test multiple sites simultaneously.

A Public Lab-led collaboration of scientists, designers, community organizers, concerned people, wetland researchers and anthropologists are currently working together to generate alternative DIY approaches to detect-

---

2   This blog illustrates patient activism around optical brighteners in detergents http://www.talkallergy.com/webdocs/yourlives/detergents.php

3   http://publiclaboratory.org/wiki/spectral-analysis
4   http://spectralchallenge.org/

ing and illustrating H₂S contamination. One of these researchers, Megan, describes her experiences developing the photographic paper tool for H_2S sensing:

I became interested in issues surrounding natural gas drilling a few years ago when the massive drilling of the Marcellus Shale began near my home in Pennsylvania. I remember going to a conference at Temple University where a panel of scientists, activists and political leaders talked about this issue. I left outraged, it was as if they were all speaking different languages. The scientists were brilliant and had all the tools to predict what would happen, but held no opinion on those predictions and could not communicate them to the public. The activists were in constant attack mode and could not listen and the politicians would only defend their own actions.

I was excited to find out about Public Laboratory while pursuing my graduate degree at Rhode Island School of Design. The Public Lab research group at RISD was just beginning to create a DIY test that could register the presence of H_2S (a toxic bi-product of natural gas drilling) in the air. The test would use regular photo paper prepared in a certain way, allowing it to be exposed to the air. Over the next few months, we made the test strips from photo paper and containers to place the strips in. We tested the difference in light exposure for each container. We read papers on the various methods of testing H_2S that were already being used by scientists in field research and adapted them to suit our needs, and met with a local air-quality testing expert.

This summer we were able to begin field testing, in collaboration with a local environmental justice group. We have completed the first experiment on an active well pad and are now in the process of running a second experiment and developing a prototype kit that can be sent out to groups and individuals who want to test their own backyard. While there is still much work to be done, the open source nature of Public Laboratory allows for information to be shared easily so that the project can move along in a more effective way, because of the amount of input received. The next step is to calibrate the color of the photo paper test strip to a quantity of H_2S in the air. (Megan McLaughlin September 2012.)

Field experiments like Megan's are a novel attempt to redress the gap between landowner's perceptions of a hazardous smell and scientific evidence required by regulators. As Megan's results illustrate, the degree of darkening of the photopaper is easily readable by non-experts and could be arranged as a map to make sources of H_2S smell evident to regulatory audiences (Horwell et al. 2005). The investigations undertaken by Megan and Josh show how citizens are attempting to harness technology to respond to many contemporary hazards that have remained imperceptible due to a lack of available research tools, misinformation and regulatory disinterest. Public Lab provides a collaborative space where individuals from all sorts of backgrounds can collaborate to generate research tools, methods, and case studies of their environments, in order to help those who are negatively impacted by hazards of industrial life on a daily basis make these threats perceptible and actionable. ■

SARA WYLIE *is a Senior Research Scientist in Northeastern University's Social Science Environmental Health Research Institute and a co-founder of Public Laboratory for Open Technology and Science.* **MEGAN MCLAUGHLIN** *is currently pursuing a masters of landscape architecture at Rhode Island School of Design.* **JOSH MCILVAIN** *lives in Kansas with his wife and two sons, and is currently pursing a masters in medical physics.*

REFERENCES

Belsito, Donald. V., et al. 2002. "Allergic contact dermatitis to detergents: a multicenter study to assess prevalence." *Journal of the American Academy of Dermatology*, 46(2):200–6.

Calnan, C. D. 1973. "Hazards of optic bleachers." *Transactions of the St. Johns Hospital Dermatolgy Society*. 59(2):275–82.

Colson, John. 2011. "Report: Hydrogen sulfide detected in air at Silt Mesa; Health official, industry doubt findings are true." *Post Independent*, July 14.

Fortun, Kim and Michael Fortun. 2005. "Scientific Imaginaries and Ethical Plateaus in Contemporary U.S. Toxicology." *American Anthropologist*, 107(1): 43–54.

Ganz, Charles. R. et al. 1975. "Accumulation and elimination studies of four detergent fluorescent whitening agents in bluegill (Lepomis macrochirus)." *Environmental Science & Technology*, 9: 738–744.

Global Commuinty Monitor. 2011. "Gassed! Citizen Investigation of Toxic Air Pollution from Natural Gas Development." *Global Community Monitor*, July 12.

Horwell, Claire.J. et al. 2004. "Evaluation of a simple passive sampling technique for monitoring volcanogenic hydrogen sulphide." *Journal of Environmental Monitoring* 6(7): 630–635.

Horwell, Claire.J. et al. 2005. "Monitoring and mapping of hydrogen sulphide emissions across an active geothermal field: Rotorua, New Zealand." *Journal of Volcanology and Geothermal Research*, 139(3–4):259–269.

Newman, Andrew. 2010. "Seventh Generation Highlights Its Chemical Free Detergent" *New York Times* December 29.

Osmundsen, P. E. 1969. "Contact dermatitis due to an optical whitener in washing products." *British Journal of Dermatology* 81(11): 799–803.

Osmundsen, P. E. and M.D Alani. 1971. "Contact allergy to an optical whitener, "CPY", in washing powders." *British Journal of Dermatology*, 85(1):61–6.

Rowe, Helen. D. 2006. "Detergents, clothing and the consumer with sensitive skin." *International Journal of Consumer Studies*, 30(4): 369–377.

Sanchez–Meza, Juan–Carlos et al. 2007. "Toxicity assessment of a complex industrial wastewater using aquatic and terrestrial bioassays Daphnia pules and Lactuca sativa." *Journal of Environmental Science & Health* 42(10):1425–1431.

Sturm, R. N, K. E. Williams, and K. J. Macek. 1975. "Fluorescent whitening agents: Acute fish toxicity and accumulation studies." *Water Research*, 9(2):211–219.

Wylie, Sarah, Jailbert, S. K. Dosemagen, and Matt Ratto. Forthcoming. "Institutions for Civic Technoscience: How Critical Making is Transforming Environmental Research". *Information Society* Special Issue on Critical Making, Wylie S, Jailbert K. and Ratto M. Eds.

JOSH'S UV DETERGENT TEST RESULTS

393nm UV

393nm UV through tap water

393nm UV through Clorox bleach

393nm UV through homemade detergent

393nm UV through Seventh Generation Free and Clear Detergent

393nm UV through All Free and Clear Detergent

Josh's results analyzed in Spectral Workbench. Compare the first image in the set, showing just UV light, to the fifth image in the set. Image five shows the UV light being absorbed by the "All Free and Clear Detergent" and resultant emission of blue light. This illustrates the presence of brighteners.

*Volunteers sit all night in a Human Landing Catch in Dar es Salaam, providing blood meals to needy local mosquitoes. **Ann H. Kelly** explores the role of volunteers' bodies in measuring the size and nature of insect-borne public health threats.*

SNARING VECTORS

ABOVE: Experimental Hut

LEFT: Human Landing Catch

NEXT PAGE: Vector Sample

On a narrow path in one of Dar es Salaam's unplanned settlements, a man sits on a wooden stool. His feet are planted squarely on top his flip-flops, a cooler and a few styrofoam cups are scattered nearby. In his mouth he holds one end of a rubber tube; the other end, a glass vial, is poised just above his shin. For the better part of the night, he will wait, his headlamp fixed on his legs, catching mosquitoes as they land on his legs attempting to feed.

The Human Landing Catch (HLC) was one of several techniques deployed by the city's Urban Malaria Control Program (UMCP) to measure the density of mosquito populations throughout Dar es Salaam. From 2004 to 2009, neighborhood vol-

unteers known as Community-Owned Resource Persons, or CORPS, were recruited to attract and collect mosquitoes during their peak biting hours (sunset to sunrise) at a number of select locations across the city. Compensated at a daily rate of three thousand Tanzanian Shillings (roughly $2.45), these participants were asked to catch mosquitoes for forty-five minutes every hour (allowing fifteen minutes to organize samples and annotate a collection log) throughout the night. Because mosquitoes were caught while seeking a blood meal, the HLC not only served as an index for vector density, but also as a parameter for malaria transmission rates. This and other researches conducted under the auspices of the UMCP sought to develop tactics of control attuned to the specific malarial dynamics of the city (Chaki et al. 2012).

The Human Landing Catch seems the stuff of imperial nightmares—global health researchers using Africans as bait (c.f. White, 1995). However, in practice, the problems with the method are perhaps more mundane. Free prophylactic treatment, regular screenings for parasites, and access to health care counter the dangers of pathogenic exposure. The real drawback of the method, according to its practitioners, is its tiresome and monotonous nature. The HLC requires focus, skill and above all stamina. But while grueling and difficult to supervise, the HLC remains a central entomological technique to estimate the size and nature of insect-borne public health threats. In the context of the UMCP, it offered a practical solution to the problem of how to monitor a residual and highly distributed vector-population. To understand the method's empirical capacity, I would like to suspend the heady ethical and biopolitical questions the HLC raises, and first ask: *How does the catcher's body relate to the task of measurement?*

In public health, the body is the definitive indicator: Its surfaces, structure, and biochemistry anticipate epidemics and locate environmental risks. The epidemiological significance of the HLC is different. Here, the human does not form part of a sample, but is rather used as a snare. The human trap is without complex mechanism or architecture; but its composition is nevertheless structured by the dialectics of predator-prey (c.f. Lévi-Strauss, 1966: 50). The material setting and set-up—back-alley, nightfall, bare legs, ankles and feet—enact an archetypical moment of man-vector contact. The fixity of the human form—aspirator in human, cups and cotton wool in hand—transforms that scenario into a means of capture. His body acts as lure, apparatus, cage and inscription device; it is an epistemic thing, providing a "surface on which apparatus and objects make contact" (Rheinberger, 2010: 217).

This take on the HLC may seem grandiose; as an experimental set up it seems on a par with swatting flies. However, if we consider the HLC as one of several devices used to elucidate mosquito dispositions and preferences, the subtleties of the method become clear. The HLC belongs to a family of devices that aim to model vector dynamics through a workable format and material versatility. Another classic example is the experimental hut—artificial homes where entomologists can model the vicissitudes of mosquito flight and indoors feeding (Kelly, 2012). While attempting to simulate natural conditions (traditional architecture, thatch walls, human sleepers) these experimental replicas of the domestic realm are structurally modified to render mosquito behaviors visible—window traps, light apertures and modular walls enable researchers to monitor and manipulate flight patterns, trenches and raised platforms keep out scavengers who might remove dead or dying mosquitoes before they can be collected. Experimental huts, like the Human Landing Catch, reflect the behavior of prey and model the intentions of the hunter; they are, in this sense, a 'lethal parody of the animal's Umwelt' (Gell, 1998: 27).

In the experimental hut too, the body is multiply configured by the experiment: The sleepers attract, catch and graphically trace the trajectory of the mosquito as it intersects with human hosts. In the experimental hut, that movement is domestic; the reciprocal exchange of parasites from mosquito to human happens within the home (Kelly, 2012). The HLC elaborates a different vectoral space: In response to years of interventions aimed at the home—indoor residual spray, household screening, ceiling boards, insecticide-treated nets—mosquitoes in Dar es Salaam are increasingly likely to feed outdoors. In fact, this behavioral shift of *Anopheles Gambiae*, its growing ability to seek human blood in the streets, was the central justification for undertaking the UMCP. Malaria risk can no longer be mapped onto a discrete intra-domiciliary space; it is distributed within, and heightened by, the vicissitudes of urban ecology—the built environment, the circuits along which water and waste circulate, the daily trajectories of permanent and transient inhabitants (c.f. Mitchell, 2002:19-54). Because mosquitos can breed in almost any body of water, malaria hot-spots can appear suddenly and anywhere—a clogged drain, a pile of tires, a newly tended garden. Reducing malaria transmission thus requires a spatially extensive and temporally intensive monitoring platform capable of tracking vector-populations as they surface and disperse in the city.

The HLC provides that necessary investigative intimacy. Residents transformed into sentinels, the CORPS' rapt attention extended the UMCPS gaze to the minute depressions, fissures, and tiny accumulations were mosquitoes proliferate. Fixed in their chairs from sunrise to sunset, the CORPS anticipates an approach to malaria control that is quite literally, *situated*. ∎

ANN H. KELLY *is a Lecturer in the Department of Sociology, Philosophy and Anthropology at the University of Exeter, Devon UK. Her work explores the production of scientific facts in Africa, with special attention to the built-environments, material artifacts, and practical labors of experimentation.*

REFERENCES

Chaki, Prosper P. et al.2012. "An affordable, quality-assured community-based system for high resolution entomological surveillance of vector mosquitoes that reflects human malaria infection risk patterns" *Malaria Journal,* 11:172, May 24. doi:10.1186/1478-4491-921.

Gell, Alfred. 1996. "Vogel's net: traps as artworks and artworks as traps." *Journal of Material Culture* 1(1):15-38.

Kelly, Ann H. 2012. The Experimental hut: Hospitable Vectors. *Journal of the Royal Anthropology Institute,* 8 (1S):145-160.

Lévi-Strauss, Claude. 1966. *The Savage Mind.* Chicago: Chicago University Press.

Mitchell, Timothy. 2002. *Rule of Experts: Egypt, TechnoPolitics, and Modernity.* Berkeley: University of California Press.

Rheinberger, Hans Jorg. 2010. *An Epistemology of the Concrete: Twentieth Century Histories of Life.* Durham & London: Duke University Press.

White, Louise. 1995. "Tsetse Visions: Narratives of Blood and Bugs in Colonial Northern Rhodesia, 1931-9." *The Journal of African History,* 36(2):219-245.

PHOTO: MUHAMMAD MAHDI KARIM

RECORDING and MONITORING

BETWEEN TWO FORMS OF SURVEILLANCE

VANESSA MANCERON argues that when naturalists take part in monitoring programs on their "local patch," they are caught between two forms surveillance: care and control.

NATURALISTS PRESENT THE SURVEILLANCE OF biodiversity through counting species and populations as a mode of knowledge that allows informed public action to bend the course of natural history. In England, such monitoring, initially pioneered under the Environmental Trusts, only became important after the publication of a governmental report "Biodiversity: The UK action plan" in 1994 that built upon the recently ratified Rio Convention.

The range of the activities unleashed under this new form of surveillance is striking: Several thousand people attempt to relentlessly inventory all the animals and plants of England in all the hidden recesses of the national territory, giving rise to huge data flows. Though the scale of coordination and research activity is a social success story, the effectiveness of the resulting inventories in inciting public action has been difficult to assess. There is a gap between the importance of the wildlife monitoring system and the invisibility of the links between statistics and effective environmental protection. I would like to pursue the idea that these inventories are devices which are partly self-sufficient. The efficacy of counting and mapping wildlife lies in the act itself. These acts of counting should therefore be seen as a way of repopulating the natural world and of dealing with the deep feelings of loss that drive amateur naturalists.

A dual form of surveillance is practiced in these spaces: pastoral (care, protection, solicitude) and governmental (security, control, economic measure, power). In this essay, I explore this duality of surveillance through fieldwork in Somerset (UK), and I focus my inquiry on amateur naturalist movements. I have observed a shift in how the relation between recording and monitoring is conceived by these naturalists that echoes the ambivalence of the very act of counting itself.

RECORDING : SURVEILLANCE AS CARE

Recording is the term commonly used by naturalists. It means recording a state of the world at a given instant, but also keeping a trace of the recorder's lived experience. Records are textual, iconographic and informatic traces which demonstrate, testify and evoke a natural history that is at the same time very personal. These records are kept with care since they are conceived as memory landmarks to reconstitute the past, both in nature and in the life of the naturalist. Recording fulfills a desire for completeness. It expresses a submission to an unknowable reality that it hopes to circumscribe. It adheres humbly and consciously to a multitude, whose profusion it patiently tries to assimilate. Naturalists compare themselves to collectors. Recording follows the gestures of collecting eggs, butterflies, insects, bones, feathers – gestures they performed in their childhood that gave them series to complete. For naturalists, collecting produces a series of facts rather than specimens, but it also accumulates things seen, touched or heard. Records are entities of numbers, paper or ink that make things present in their absence.

This engagement with recording also takes shape in the spatial and temporal aspects of the personal lives of naturalists. At a spatial level, recording implies exploring every corner of a territory shared with other living beings. In the English countryside, where many people originating from the city live, familiarity with local places is part of a feeling of belonging that relies less on filiation than on the production of a "home". This familiar territory, like a garden or a street, is usually made close to one's house. Naturalists call this territory "local patch". It can be a piece of land, a path, a trajectory. This territory is built by walking and counting, with eyes and ears oriented towards certain living beings rather than others. These patches are not landscapes but assemblages of colors, forms, textures and sounds and exist for the naturalist recorder an abstract rather than figurative representation. This attachment to places does not refer to human sociability, which is perceived as unstable, but instead to a non-human population. Those who play the role of ancestors are the earlier naturalists who have walked on the same paths, and whose records are sometimes kept preciously in their home.

Inventories are therefore spatial, temporal and social connectors. More than a pastime, they are a form of affective and sensitive engagement of individuals in the world (Lorimer, 2008). Maps and inventories are means to re-populating nature. Counting is a way to make sure that all known living beings are there, as a shepherd counts his cattle. Counting those who remain is also a way to bring new beings into existence: It is a form of insurance and reinsurance. It domesticates and breeds the wild.

MONITORING: SURVEILLANCE AS CONTROL

Monitoring is the term used by conservation managers and by scientists to describe a method of recording that is endowed with a program assigned to a scientific protocol that is theoretically reproducible and reliable. Monitoring is linked to surveillance, vigilance and control. This type of gathering is used for management planning, including the administration of territories dedicated to conservation. Trusts, including Wildlife Trusts as the county level, have been key enablers of "monitoring" networks that have been set up since two decades. This particular brand of locally anchored participatory devices could network naturalists who were observing plants or birds by themselves or in small groups.

In this context, inventories are defined as devices to measure acceptable variables in relation to a previously determined desired state of nature. These inventories can be read as norms transformed into figures, and they act as whistleblowers in case of a threat to a site or to a species. They can also provide metrics that allow protection projects to be evaluated by funding organizations. These counting practices are situated at the articulation of, on one side, a planning-oriented government that requires indicators to assess administration oriented results. On the other, the practices support a strategic mode of governance interested in potential interactions between society and the environment (urbanization and biodiversity, for instance), and relying on statistics to support and strengthen local, national and international negotiations

TOP
Volunteers prepare for a day of observing.

LEFT
A naturalist spies nature.

to win institutional and financial support for preservation efforts.

The now common use of atlases which provide tool to enable users of biodiversity information to find, access and visualize data on plants and animals brings to light the emergence of risk mapping as a mode of government. Mapping gains authority and credibility not only through its objectifying strength, but also through a series of actions that aim to acknowledge the legitimacy of the map and endow it with an operating capacity. The atlas designed to inform decision-makers about risk objectifies, in a strong visual way, facts that must trigger consent and stimulate reactions at the local and global levels. Holes on the map representing the disappearance of species produce anxiety among key stakeholders and help to make a case for action.

Counting thus means working for an institutional power. Naturalist amateurs call themselves "volunteers". This term refers to a form of enrollment in an "army" of observers at the service of nature. The use of this expression attempts to evoke patriotic tones since the goal is to mobilize efforts to save local species and promote biodiversity as part of broader efforts at preserving territorial and historical integrity. This public injunction has led naturalist amateurs to organize the recruitment and training of walkers, to renounce previously widespread practices of free roaming and keen observation of their patches, to dedicate time to natural reserves, to collect their data without receiving anything back, and to keep for themselves a very individualized and localized record of their knowledge.

This process of promoting monitoring, databases, standardized set of techniques and atlases gives rise to resistances, avoidance, and sometimes conflicts with the environmentalist bodies (Ellis & Waterton, 2004). Despite occasional setbacks, the inventorying system it produces continues to develop and grow. Indeed, the desire to inventory lies to the moral sense of duty that comes out of an ascetic ethics. Naturalist occupations enter the category of "pastime". These practices take on both pleasant and useful qualities, but also require a strong personal discipline. Naturalism was promoted during the Victorian era as a form of education and personal accomplishment that endow the practitioner with a "godly" and sane morality (Allen, 1976).

Today, the feeling of duty comes from adherence to a political community through trust institutions, which attempt to enact change by representing their work as a force at the service of society, an adviser of governments, and a civic movement. Data cumulated from individual gatherers in a central database makes possible the construction of an image of a totality that provides a visual or spatial representation of the evolution and the distribution of all England's species. This totality is the result of a social network and everyone feels proud to take part in the national effort.

CONCLUSION

Biodiversity monitors oscillate between two forms of surveillance. On one side, surveillance is a form of care for the well-being of non-humans they take in their charge. Counting and making inventories often constitutes a co-operative, affective and descriptive form of surveillance. Naturalist amateurs consider themselves as lookouts or watchmen. They know their "local patch" well and feel the duty to protect and care for it. From their point of view watching means being careful vigilant. Their relationship to local wildlife bears a similarity to the way a gardener tends to his garden or a shepherd presides over his flock.

On the other side, surveillance is a form of control over the territory and over other humans in order to guarantee the development of best preservation practices. In that context, the amateurs also conceive their role as the equivalent of wardens or guards. Counting and making inventories refer to the concept of "local eyes", a relationship to the natural world that is an equivalent to the "neighborhood watch". This form of sentinel is norma-

tive and prescriptive. The naturalists are amateurs in both senses of the term: they are volunteers and members of a political community, but they also have attachment to a territory that they share with other living beings. The coexistence of these two dispositions explains why the system of surveillance holds together.

For naturalists, inventories belong to three registers: a charity activity, a way to fight against urban projects and a sentinel of species extinction. This last aspect involves the act of sensing danger. Naturalists know in detail their local patches. This knowledge so intimately linked to place corresponds to an individual measurement of species presence in the natural field. Naturalists are considered as eye witnesses by conservationist bodies, but not as specialists dedicated to sending reliable warning signals of species extinction. In fact, the warning device is the monitoring system itself : the individual act of seeing and counting, subsequently gathered and interested into massive national data systems, is the only method capable of sounding an alarm and declaring that a crisis has been triggered. In this sense, the "canary in the mine" trope refers to the decline of a particular species. When a familiar bird is declared to be in danger, the bodies and groups focused on wildlife conservation give an alert to the rest of the world, including to national authorities. Interpreted in this way, the recording of a bird species disappearing, like the canary in the mine, alerts humans that the future of wildlife, as well as their own destiny on planet Earth, are imperiled. ■

VANESSA MANCERON *is anthropologist and researcher in the Laboratoire d'ethnologie et de sociologie comparative at the National Center of Scientific Research (CNRS) in Paris. She is the author of* Une terre en partage. Liens et rivalités dans une société rurale *and the editor of "Les animaux de la discorde," a special issue of* Ethnologie Française.

I AM GRATEFUL to Frédéric Keck for his translation work and to the participants in the Borchard Fondation Colloquium at Missilac who raised comments in discussion.

BIBLIOGRAPHY

Allen, David Elliston. 1976. *The Naturalist in Britain. A social history.* London: Allen Lane, Penguin Books Hardcover Edition.

Ellis, Rebecca and Claire Waterton. 2004. "Volunteers and Citizenship. Environmental citizenship in the making: The participation of volunteers naturalist in UK biological recording and biodiversity policy." *Science and Public Policy*, 31(2):95-105.

Lorimer, Jamie. 2008. "Counting Corncrakes: The Affective Science of the UK Corncrake Census" *Social Studies of Science*, 38(3):377-405.

SERUM AS SENTINEL

Does frozen blood send an 'as yet unknown' signal? **Joanna Radin** describes how serological epidemiology has made the recent past into a sentinel of the near future.

In 2009 numerous reports of a potentially dangerous flu activated existing global systems of surveillance. As public health officials attempted to characterize the strain associated with the outbreak they turned towards a unique historical resource to help determine the scale of preparations necessary for managing a possible epidemic: freezers filled with blood.

Blood serum samples from human and non-human populations collected and preserved at labs around the world years earlier were compared to the 2009 flu strain. The goal was to determine changes in the virus and to see what immunological traces it had left in the serum. Such knowledge would yield important clues as to what was in store. Had the 2009 virus evolved resistance to existing medicines? Would available vaccines afford adequate protection to those in need? The story of how old blood serum became the substrate for this kind of epidemiological sentinel system is central to understanding present-day strategies for anticipating and mitigating threats to population health.

In the early 1950s Yale polio researcher John Rodman Paul and his colleagues began to publicize an approach to tracking disease they called "serological epidemiology." This new method represented a marriage of the techniques of the biological lab—specifically, the analysis of serum, the liquid component of blood—to the practice of epidemiology, the study of patterns of infection and immunity. To be sure, the techniques available for analyzing blood serum in the 1950s were not new. Serology had been in use by immunologists since the 19th century and physical anthropologists had been working since the early 20th century

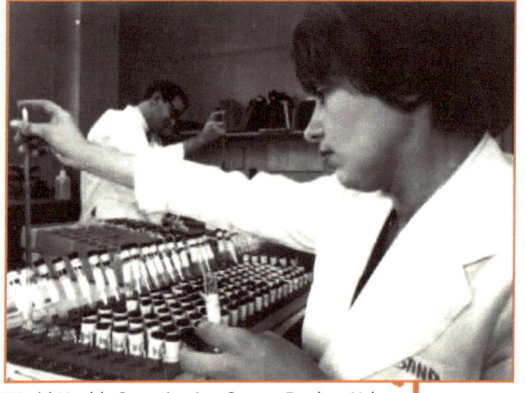

World Health Organization Serum Bank at Yale.

to detect and map variable genetic traits such as the ABO blood groups.

However, Paul realized that once collected, such blood could be preserved and therefore made available for new uses in the future. He argued that to realize its full potential as a sentinel system, serological epidemiology required: (1) the ability to analyze and subsequently reanalyze—for purposes other than that for which they were originally collected—large numbers (hundreds of thousands) of unique blood samples and (2) the long-term, cold-storage of such specimens along with information about the persons from whom they were collected.[1]

Serological epidemiology gained momentum due to a number of factors, including improvements in technologies of cold storage such as mechanical refrigeration and liquid nitrogen; an increased recognition of the relevance of the lab to matters of public health; unprecedented access to air travel which facilitated the collection and circulation of blood samples; new computing technology for handling large amounts of data; and the creation of new international organizations, such as the World Health Organization (WHO), with the authority to standardize protocols to ensure that there was consistency between labs in the ways they maintained and analyzed blood.[2]

In 1958, a clutch of experts—including Paul's collaborator at

---

1   For a concise overview of serological epidemiology as it was understood at mid-century see (Payne 1965).

2   Practices related to the creation of related, large-scale repositories of frozen blood for population research are discussed in (Radin 2013).

Yale, Dorothy Hortstmann—convened at the WHO's headquarters in Geneva to draft a plan for implementing serological epidemiology on a global scale. Influenza weighed heavily on the minds of the participants. Many of those in attendance, including Horstmann, had lived through the deadly 1918 "Spanish Flu" pandemic. That flu—which would later be identified as an H1N1 strain—was linked to more deaths than World War I. At the time, however, little was known about the causes of influenza, let alone its biology. The participants at the Geneva meeting believed that serological epidemiology would play a critical role in attempts to harness emerging insights in biomedicine for the management of future outbreaks.

The following year, in 1959, the WHO published their recommendations in a report titled "Immunological and Haematological Surveys." Pointing to the case of the 1918 flu pandemic, the authors stated:

> If samples of the sera collected in these surveys are stored in such a way as to preserve antibodies, it will be possible to examine them in the future and so to determine the past history of infections as yet unknown and to follow more clearly the changing pattern of communicable diseases all over the world

(WHO, 1959).

"AS YET UNKNOWN" would be a familiar refrain to those who supported the creation, maintenance, and use of these accumulated frozen blood samples. The phrase alluded to the growing conviction that blood harbored traces of biological risks not yet understood by public health workers. The power of serological epidemiology stemmed from two related ways of imagining the uses of old, cold blood: to anticipate known risks and to locate the origins of unanticipated and emergent threats.

In the decades that followed, storehouses of blood grew as samples were collected from a wide range of bodies including members of communities that had recently experienced epidemics, military recruits, Peace Corps volunteers, students, immigrants, and so-called "primitive peoples." The awareness that infections sometimes jumped from a non-human to a human host also led epidemiologists to begin collecting blood from the domesticated and wild animals that lived amidst some of these populations.

In the 1980s, frozen blood samples collected during the early years of this push to create long-term repositories were used to make a case for the African origins of HIV. Historian Edward Hooper has described how two researchers, Arno Motulsky and Moses Schanfield, re-analyzed hundreds of old specimens and found one, collected near Leopoldville in 1959—the same year that the WHO report on "Immunological and Haematological Surveys" was published—that tested positive on all of the then-available antibody tests associated with HIV (Hooper, 1999).

Around the same time, utilizing a DNA amplification technique known as polymerase chain reaction (PCR), epidemiologists also began to incorporate genomics into their analytic repertoire. They searched old blood for fragments of DNA that could and have since informed studies of infectious diseases, including H1N1, H5N1 (bird flu), and SARS. Recently, some scientists have begun to mine old human blood for the DNA of malaria. The hope is that this new application of genomics will yield clues about when and how the plasmodium evolved resistance to drugs that had previously been effective in preventing infection. Still other researchers are defrosting old blood samples to gain purchase on the genetics of a huge range of complex conditions, ranging from diabetes to schizophrenia.

As blood samples continue to be accumulated in freezers around the world, it is possible to say that the serological epidemiological system formalized in 1959 has realized, if not exceeded, the intentions of Paul, Horstmann, and others who anticipated the need for new strategies to manage disease risks. In 2009, for instance, serological epidemiology—which by then encompassed older immunological tests as well as new genomic ones—helped public health workers to determine that "swine flu" would not be as deadly as the 1918 flu.

At the same time, certain people whose blood is stored as part of this surveillance system have sought to have it removed from the ongoing and increasingly lucrative enterprise of revealing new forms of embodied risk. In the decades since the first round of serological epidemiological collections were assembled, blood—including some that was collected under the auspices of WHO's protocols—has been at the center of potent debates about patenting the body, the racialization of genomic medicine, and abuses of human research subjects. Some communities, such as the Havasupai in Arizona and the Yanomami in the Amazon, have demanded that their blood be removed from biomedicine's freezers. In doing so, they have demonstrated that new uses for old blood have been accompanied by new forms of exclusion or injury. In other words, though scientists initially understood this blood to be frozen, they have discovered that attitudes about the ends to which it can and should be put are far from fixed.

While these kinds of biosocial harms were not among those anticipated by the architects of serological epidemiology, they should not be faulted for failing to accurately predict the future. The system of surveillance they forged was designed to accommodate *known* unknowns: the likely emergence of new viruses. Looking forward to great advances in biomedicine, they did not consider that those advances would inevitably be accompanied by new ideas about what it means to be a subject of biomedical research. It is in this sense that present-day debates around the appropriate uses of old frozen blood have come to serve as a sentinel of emerging problems of ethics as well as of epidemiology. ■

JOANNA RADIN *is an Assistant Professor of History of Medicine at Yale University. She is currently at work on a book about frozen blood.*

REFERENCES

Hooper, Edward. 1999. *The River: A Journey to the Source of HIV and AIDS.* New York: Little, Brown and Company.

Payne, Anthony M. 1965. "Serum Surveys." *The Milbank Memorial Fund Quarterly*, 4(2):345–350.

Radin, Joanna. 2013. "Latent Life: Concepts and Practices of Human Tissue Preservation in the International Biological Program." *Social Studies of Science.* (April 9th) DOI: 10.1177/0306312713476131

World Health Organization. 1959. "Immunological and Haematological Surveys." Technical Report Series no. 181, Geneva, Switzerland.

SENTINEL ORGANISMS

'They look out for the environment!'

Under what conditions can animals and plants be considered as good sentinels for an environment? *Christelle Gramaglia* looks at the uses of shells to detect water pollution.

THANKS TO THE DEVELOPMENT OF NEW METHODS at the interface of ecology and chemistry first pioneered in the 1970s, environmental sensors such as sentinel organisms are today used to detect signs of disturbances that remain indiscernible to humans, providing specific data on the noxiousness of pollutants.[1] Many animals and plants have since been tested and "enrolled" (Akrich *et al.* 2006) in environmental monitoring programs, making it possible to lower the threshold for detecting toxins in air, soil and water, and allowing investigations on the effects of low doses of particular pollutants on the environment. As a result of new funding and attention to the issue, lab and outdoor experiments multiplied in subsequent years.

Ecotoxicologists study the potential environmental impact of pollutants by observing how they affect chosen organisms at the physiological, cellular and molecular levels. They do not aim at producing data about pollutants' impact on humans directly. However, their findings on the contamination of plants and animals guide authorities who decide whether catching and consuming specific plants and animals should be regulated or not. For instance, in our case study, in the Gironde estuary, downstream the River Lot (Southwestern France), ecotoxicologists' findings on heavy metal concentrations in aquatic species led to a ban on the consumption of some fish and shellfish.

This paper examines scientific uses of the *Corbicula fluminae* as a sentinel organism to detect zinc and cadmium pollution in a lab experiment and along the River Lot. It will give us the opportunity to discuss the role of plants and animals in environmental monitoring, and explore how the very concept of "sentinel" takes on new meanings when applied to the surveillance of risks.

THE TOXIC LEGACY OF PAST INDUSTRIAL ACTIVITIES

Cadmium is naturally present in small quantities in most metalliferous ore. Its physical and chemical properties are numerous. It is highly resistant to corrosion and heat and not easily soluble in water. These characteristics make it an ideal material to add to domestic household items such as batteries, paint and plastics. While its industrial uses expanded in the 20th century, its release into the environment started in the 19th century with the production of

---

1   Wilhelm Nylander, a Finnish botanist working for the Museum of Natural History in Paris was one pioneer. He mapped air pollution based on his interpretations of lichen distribution in the Luxembourg gardens. He called the plants "hygiometers" as they helped him assess the salubrity of a location (1869). However, he worked mostly alone and no other scientist of his time continued his research. Animals like canaries may have been used as sensors for hazards in everyday practice, but their contribution was not investigated scientifically.

zinc. For each ton of zinc that is smelted, about 3 kilograms of cadmium residue is also produced. Unlike zinc, which is necessary for the healthy functioning of human, animal and plant metabolisms, cadmium is highly toxic even at low doses. It can generate bone, kidney, liver and reproductive disorders (Nordberg 2004).

In Aveyron, the aftermath of 150 years of zinc metallurgy activities is not immediately discernible. With its rural surroundings and its 1,400 inhabitants, the town of Viviez has managed to keep a quiet atmosphere despite the presence of several factories and wastelands. The water of the Riou Mort, which runs through the town and then into the River Lot a few kilometers downstream, looks quite limpid. The apparent cleanliness of the waters belies the fact that high concentrations of heavy metals released by the local zinc factory over the past century are still trapped in the riverbed. The toxins can also be found in the River Lot sediments and affect the quality of the whole water system up to the Gironde estuary. The confluence of the rivers is currently being closely monitored by scientists.

Ecotoxicologists study pollution in order to assess its noxiousness on aquatic plants and animals. To this end, they have designed new experiments to obtain data showing how different heavy metals affect aquatic life, irrespective of the quantity or chemical status of these metals. To help them overcome difficulties involved in understanding complex phenomena which the human eye and instruments alone cannot fully grasp, they chose to "enroll" a heterogeneous cohort of life forms based on their specific ability to detect zinc and cadmium at low doses and to survive despite the damage caused by these pollutants.

MONITORING CONTAMINATION

The scientists I met said they rapidly realized that a mollusk named *Corbicula,* an invasive species originating from Asia, could help them understanding better the dynamics and effects of pollution, which technical tools had been unable to capture. These animals, whose biology is now well known, live at the interface between river water and sediments. Their breathing and feeding activities involve filtering high quantities of water and ingesting the pollutants present in it.

Working with *Corbicula* has several practical advantages. They are easy to find in lakes which are not contaminated by cadmium. They are not expensive to breed. They can be transported and kept in the animal house in the lab and require minimum care. They can survive for up to six weeks without food provided they have a supply of oxygenated water, including tap water. Their food, a microscopic alga called *Scenedesmus*, can be cultivated without difficulty either. *Corbicula* adapt perfectly to the artificial rivers used in the lab made of ordinary PVC pipes, gravel and water. Their life cycle is not as short as that of *Drosophila*, but it is still short enough to enable scientists to observe their development and reproduction in a time adapted to the rhythm of laboratory work (Kohler 1993). If all mollusks can detect heavy metals in water at low doses and generally react to their presence, all species are not equally resistant. The distinctive feature of *Corbicula* is their ability to survive both zinc and cadmium at the same time. Except when the dose is lethal, they can assimilate and concentrate these substances. However, after exposure to these substances they grow smaller and their behaviors are impaired. These signs provide ecotoxicologists with valuable information about the toxic effects of heavy metals. Their distinguishing traits make them rather attractive animals, i.e. "good candidates to act as lab and sentinel organisms".

The scientists I observed in the lab and in the field call on *Corbicula* in different ways in their experiments. The organisms are handled and treated carefully because their performance depends directly on their well-being. In the simplified but controlled conditions of the lab, ecotoxicologists put them in artificial rivers in which they can introduce heavy metals progressively to examine their impact. In situ, *Corbicula* are placed in cages and immersed in rivers such as the Riou Mort. They are carefully transported to the field in a cooler filled with water oxygenated by a pump before being placed in groups of 25 in different locations both upstream and downstream from the zinc factory in Viviez. They are usually picked up 15 days later by the technician and PhD students who brought them there. Each group of mollusks is kept in a labeled bag before being taken back to the lab. In the dissection room, they are cut into three pieces. The gills are separated from the viscera and the soft body because cadmium impacts them differently: the gills are directly in contact with the water and toxins, while the viscera have a high accumulating potential. This preparation facilitates later interpretation as data obtained from each part can be compared (Lynch 1988). Animal pieces are either analyzed immediately or frozen for later analyses.

Physiological, biomolecular or genetic assays can then be performed. The *Corbicula* are weighed, numbered and crushed. Spectrometric analyses of the soft bodies, viscera and gills enable the measurement of the quantity of cadmium filtered and concentrated by the organisms at one location. Other tests are achieved by mercury saturation to measure the rate of metallothionein, a cell protein produced by the liver to trap heavy metals and thus reduce their toxicity. This protein, being directly correlated with their ingestion, is a biomarker, i.e. an indicator of the presence of heavy metals. Damage to DNA can also be visualized by polymerase chain reaction. The structure of uncontaminated genes can then be compared to those exposed to pollution, making legible new evidence of the toxins' effects on aquatic life.

Through these experiments, ecotoxicologists showed that *Corbicula* could not survive very long in the highly polluted zones immediately downstream from Viviez. When moving down the Riou Mort, the bioavailability of heavy metals decreases and the mollusks manage to cope, although they are smaller and their reproductive functions are compromised. They display other signs of serious contamination, including a higher rate of cadmium and metallothionein in the body and genetic abnormalities (Andres *et al.* 1999, Baudrimont *et al.* 1999). Experiments demonstrated that the impacts of the heavy metals decreased downstream in the River Lot up to the Gironde estuary. In the estuary, despite the distance from Viviez, the presence of salty marine water increased bioavailability of toxins and risk of contamination for aquatic life.

WHY THE SENTINELS' POINT OF VIEW MATTERS

The *Corbicula* do things that humans and most machines cannot do. They "look out for the environment continuously" as one ecotoxicologist told me—a task that would otherwise require expensive and difficult to maintain technical equipment. Nonetheless, the mollusks should not be considered as mere tools. They are "unfree partners, whose differences and similarities to human beings, to one another, and to other organisms are crucial to the work of the lab" (Haraway 2008: 72). They are collected in lakes before being installed in rivers like the Riou Mort and the Lot. Their efficiency in detecting heavy metals is related to the fact that they come from similar aquatic ecosystems which they can speak for. The success of the experiments depends on the safe transfer of the mollusks to the experiment sites. All disturbances to the specimens must be minimized to isolate the ones caused by pollutants. For this reason, paying attention to their specific needs, i.e. learning to understand what matters for them, is a crucial part of scientific work (Gramaglia and Sampaio da Silva 2012).

Yet, the notion of model organism should be distinguished from that of sentinel organism. Model animals are manufactured in the lab and for the lab. They are cut off from any kind of environment they could have lived in to be used as proxy. Their point of view on the phenomena at stake is not to be taken into account. Whether sentinel organisms are "enrolled" in monitoring protocols and surveillance tasks which efficiency depends a great deal on their embeddedness in specific places and their ability to express preferences.

The military term for soldiers posted at the outskirts of a given territory applies well to the *Corbicula* installed in cages at various points of the Riou Mort and the River Lot. The reason mollusks can complete their assigned task is because they are part in a network dedicated to the surveillance of hazards. They stand for their locations. Knowledge about pollution is produced through the gathering of information emanating from the different stations (and also different species which may have different preferences). It is assembled in the lab operating as a "center of calculation" (Latour 1987). The contrast between the upstream situation and the downstream one brings evidence of damage into view. This comparison can also reveal unexpected phenomena, such as the fact that heavy metals like cadmium affects the Gironde estuary 400 km from the contamination point since toxic effects increase when fresh and brackish water meet. Monitoring environmental hazards with the help of sentinel organisms and collective sensing devices provides scientists with insights on the changing geography of pollution and the variable effects of low doses of toxins on a large territory.

However, the figure of the sentinel should be distinguished from that of the whistle blower too. The latter is often understood as a professional breaking the rules of confidentiality applying to his/her domain of expertise to denounce a hazard, therefore speaking out against a collective he/she is related to. By contrast, a sentinel is a part of an existing surveillance device, whether institutionalized or not. Its efficiency depends on the degree of integration in a network allowing coordination, but also the exchange and processing of information. The actions of both the sentinel and whistle blower figures can be regarded as collective achievements involving humans and non-humans, but in the case of the second figure, the alert is an act of dissociation.[2]

POLLUTION, ESPECIALLY IN ITS CHRONIC AND ACCU-mulative forms, is difficult to understand. The effects of toxins depend on a plurality of factors: the chemical status of the pollutants as well as the circumstances and the biology of the species affected by them. If a new form of localized/distributed vigilance involving different forms of life is needed to better anticipate and document the negative consequences of our actions, such a systematic vigilance requires not confining ourselves with existing norms of exposure but, instead, building surveillance networks once an alert is confirmed to capture early warnings of hazards. This new localized/distributed system could work, provided we pay close attention to the messages different sentinels carry about themselves, and reflect on what this information means for the environment we share with them. ■

CHRISTELLE GRAMAGLIA *is a sociologist. She works as a research professor at the Montpellier Institute for the sciences and technologies of the environment and agriculture (IRSTEA).*

---

2   Evidence for tension between the two can be found in the work of Cordelia Hesse-Honegger, a Swiss science illustrator who started documenting damages caused by the aftermath of Chernobyl disaster to insects' morphology in Western Europe. Raffles (2010) tells us that Hesse-Honegger's first accounts were dismissed on the ground that she had not observed a control group, nor had she collected enough data to allow statistically significant findings matching academic standards. Her aesthetic way of portraying insects' deformity magnified their singularity too much, according to scientists who refused to consider the information on irradiation her specimens were bearing as relevant. While her later research responded to these criticisms by providing a larger set of data, she regretted that the insects on her pictures were not acknowledged as sentinels capable of monitoring genetic damages affecting potentially many life forms. Her isolation and outsider status made it even more difficult for her to be heard.

REFERENCES:

Akrich, Madeleine, Michel Callon, and Bruno Latour. 2006. "*Sociologie de la traduction. Textes fondateurs.*" Paris: Presses de l'Ecole des mines.

Andres, Sandrine, Magalie Baudrimont, Yvon Lapaquellerie et. al. 1999. "Field transplantation of the freshwater bivalve Corbicula fluminea along a polymetallic contamination gradient (River Lot, France) – Part I: Geochemical characteristics of the sampling sites and cadmium and zinc bioaccumulation kinetics." *Environmental Toxicology and Chemistry*, 18(11):2462-2471.

Baudrimont, Magalie, Sandrine Andres, Jacqueline Metivaud, et. al. 1999. "Field transplantation of the freshwater bivalve Corbicula fluminea along a polymetallic contamination gradient (River Lot, France) Part II: Metallothionein response to metal exposure: a field illustration of the metal spillover theory" *Environmental Toxicology and Chemistry*, 18(11):2472-2477.

Gramaglia, Christelle and Delaine Sampaio da Silva. 2012. "Researching water quality with non-humans. An ANT Account." In J.H. Passoth, B. Peuker, M. Michael Schillmeier (eds) *Agency without Actors?: New Approaches to Collective Action.* Routledge: London: 178-195.

Haraway, Donna. J. 2008. *When species meet.* Minneapolis: University of Minnesota Press.

Kohler, Robert. 1993. "Drosophila: A life in the Laboratory." *Journal of the History of Biology*, 26(2):281-310.

Latour, Bruno. 1987. *Science in Action: How to Follow Scientists and Engineers through Society.* Cambridge, MA: Harvard University Press.

Lynch, Michael. 1988. "Sacrifice and the transformation of the animal body into a scientific object. Laboratory culture and ritual practice in the neurosciences." *Social studies of science*, 18(2):265-289.

Nordberg, F. 2004. "Cadmium and health in the 21st Century – historical remarks and trends for the future." *BioMetals*, 17(5):485-489.

Nylander, Wilhelm. 1866. "Les Lichens du Jardin du Luxembourg." *Bulletin of the Society of Botany*, 13:364-371.

Raffles, Hugh. 2010. *Insectopedia.* New York: Vintage Books

This study was funded by the French National Agency for Research (ANR project Re-Syst 08-CES-014). Interviews were conducted by Delaine Sampaio da Silva and I with researchers and lab staff from the GEEMA/AE team at the University of Bordeaux (France) who agreed to be observed and questioned.

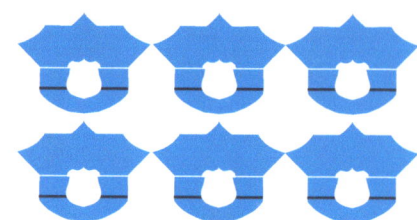

FROM SENSORS TO SENTINEL

PRESSURE AND DEPRESSION IN CRIME STATISTICS

While policemen watch out for public security, psychologists watch out for the mental health of policemen. **EMMANUEL DIDIER** looks at these two different uses of statistical data.

WHAT IS THE DISTINCTION between sensors and sentinels? Both have the capacity to sense danger, but while the sensor translates potential threats into numbers, the sentinel sends out early warning signals. For Gabriel Tarde, professor of sociology in the College de France at the turn of the XIXth century, societies indeed had sense organs: their statistical bureaus (Didier 2010). He argued that sensations were all quantitative, even when belonging to an individual person, and that this statistical character was only more visible when related to entire societies because the senses of these collectives were still retarded compared to an individual human organism. When statistics and societies develop, according to Tarde, the gap will disappear, and there will be no more difference between an individual ear and juridical statistics:

> "A statistical bureau might be compared to an eye or ear. [...] Let us hope that the day will come when the representative or legislator who is called upon to reform the judiciary or the penal code and yet who is, hypothetically, ignorant of juridical statistics, will be as rare and inconceivable a being as a blind omnibus driver or a deaf orchestral leader would be to-day. I might freely say, then, that each of our senses gives us, in its own way and from its special point of view, the statistics of the external world."
>
> (Tarde 1903, 135)

For Tarde, one of the very first things that societies have sensed statistically was crime and insecurity, the major social danger of his time. Contemporary societies produce more and more crime statistics, up to the point that they sometimes seem to appear in the world on their own. The visionary Tarde wrote "a time may come when upon the accomplishment of every social event a figure will at once issue forth automatically, so to speak, to take its place on the statistical registers" (*idem*, 167). Tarde's prophecy of a society equipped with sensors may soon be realized.

But the automaticity of the registration of crime statistics initially envisioned by Tarde appears nowadays to be an illusion. Most of these statistics are produced by the police who, right after any action they have taken, account statistically for it. In this case, the sensor is thus not the statistical bureau alone, but the beat policeman who wanders in the street, demonstrates his presence, and intervenes when necessary – all of which is supposed to produce figures. The problem is that, as every cop and every criminologist knows, it is frightening to fight against crime. The risk of being hit, shot, etc. is high, and the risk of being sanctioned by the brass if misbehavior is reported is even higher.

Thus, policemen are caught between two fires: the social danger they are supposed to fight, sense and report to the bureau and from there to the entire society, and the personal danger they perceive. These two types of sensing produce ten-

sions and contradictions in the behavior of the sensor. To escape personal danger, cops often have the tendency to do as little as possible, and even to ignore actual crime when possible.

This is why management puts pressure on them. The last tool that it designed to this end employs statistics itself, and this new system has produced strange effects. In the 1990s, William Bratton, then the Police Commissioner of the NYPD, drew from management books, especially Hammer and Champy (1993) and Osborne and Gaeblers (1992) (who were themselves influenced by Wilson (1989), the author of the famous broken-windows theory) ideas that led to the creation of COMPSTAT, a new policing organization that won the Innovations in American Government Award from the Ford Foundation and the John F. Kennedy School of Government at Harvard University. In the new protocols implemented under COMPSTAT, the precinct commanders gather their data and must explain, in front of their own chief, how they responded to the reported crimes in their precinct. They are asked to analyze and use for themselves, as managers, the data that they have collected. In management term, commanders are made accountable for the decrease of crime in their precinct, and must be able to show that they have taken initiatives. All of this must be done through statistics collected and analyzed according to COMPSTAT standards. If not, their careers are at risk.

"Reward and punishment were based

New York City Subway ■ Felonies and ■ Robberies
A chart published in Kelling and Coles (1996, 152) to
assess the positive effect of **COMPSTAT** on New York
City crime. Source : (Eterno and Silverman 2010).

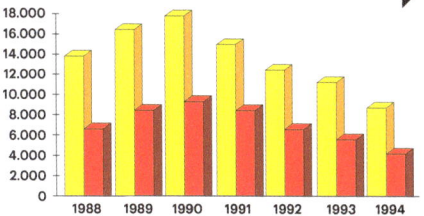

	Retired before 1995	Retired 1995-2001	Retired 2002+	For 2002: Percentage answering 3+ to "how often?"
... changed to make numbers look better	30.2%	34.9%	55.6%	90.8%
... not taking report when should have	28.2%	32.2%	46.7%	82.8%
... changing words to downgrade	25.3%	28.0%	50.8%	85.7%

Activity of the Psychological Support Operational Unit
The data was given to the article author during the
interview.

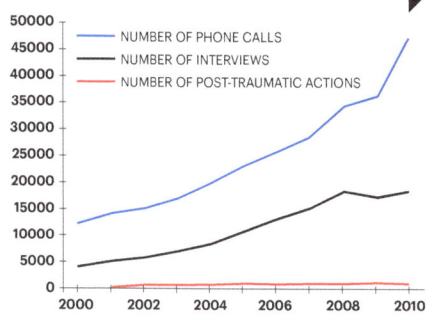

on performance and both were distributed swiftly: while more than 75% of the precinct commanders were replaced within 18 months, the participants also witnessed promotions at an unprecedented rate" (O'Connell 119) wrote one of Bratton's assistants.

The pressure put on cops in order to improve their ability to fight crime appeared to work as crime sunk dramatically in those days in NYC. When seeing government statistics from the period, observers even spoke about a "miracle".

THE SUCCESS WAS SO NOTICEABLE that a great number of polices in other parts of the US and around the whole world imitated NYPD's COMPSTAT model. Baltimore implemented a similar system under the name of Citystat (which is seen in the TV series *The Wire*) and France imported the technique in 2000 in the hope that crime would go down as much as it had in NYC. As time went by, the constant accountability and initiative that COMPSTAT requires from police officers, commanders and under, caused unpredictable effects on the careers of those implementing this model and on their work. These were not exactly the same in France and in the US.

First, new pressures created by the technique induced officers to game the numbers. It is sometimes easier to cheat the report than to actually do something against crime. One classic way to do this is to downgrade complaints. For example, someone comes in the police headquarter and reports a rape. The problem might be that the police do not want the rape rate associated with their station to rise, so they record the reported incident as a sexual assault, which is not a crime but a felony. As a result, this particular event does not enter the crime category and resources attributed to investigating and solving the crime are diminished. The police have better results, but crime paradoxically becomes easier to commit without detection. A distortion in reality appears.

In France, a controversy about the truthfulness of the crime statistical reports has steadily grown since the 1990s between the police on the one hand and social scientists and activists on the other (Didier 2011). In the US, the first whistle-blower alerting the public to the rampant problem of underreporting was Adrian Schoolcraft, an officer in the NYPD. He recorded secretly all his interactions with his chiefs during several months, and released the tapes in May 2010 to the *Village Voice*. These tapes showed many instances of police misconduct and manipulation of the crime report data. He is now in the process of suing the NYPD for intimidation.

Schoolcraft's claims were bolstered by further research, when Eterno and Silverman (2010), a former cop and a sociologist, designed a survey in which retired officers were given the chance to anonymously declare any "unethical behavior"

Eliane Theillaumas in her office in Paris

they might have engaged in because of the pressure created by the COMPSTAT statistical requirements. Their report showed that more than 50% of the officers who retired after 2002 declare having changed their reports to make figures look better.

These sociologists and their survey can be called sentinels, because they reveal an unpredicted danger: pressure put on police officers disturbs the reports that they make. This effect, called the "Goodhart law", states: "any observed statistical regularity will tend to collapse once pressure is placed upon it for control purposes" (Chrystal et al. 2001). Sentinels come into play when sensors are disturbed and biased by pressure.

But pressure might not only lead to cheating. It can also cause people to fall into a depression. When individuals have to make constant choices under the constraint of being efficient, they sometimes have a nervous breakdown (Ehrenberg 2000). The suicide of a young female officer in France in 2011 who left a letter where she explicitly accused the pressure of the statistics as one of the burdens she could not cope with is a disastrous example of the side effects of statistical pressure.

Thus, after importing COMPSTAT from the US, French management made adaptations to it because of their awareness of psychological dangers. The French version enlarged the "Psychological Support Operational Unit" (PSOU) that had been created a few years before. Michel Gaudin, who at the time was deputy director of national police, put Eliane Theillaumas in charge of overseeing the implementation of the newly expanded French PSOU.

Initially a teacher, she pursued an MA in psychology while working full-time. She was then hired as a recruiting agent for the police, but thought it would be interesting to use her skills to care for cops' psychological wounds. After hearing that there were psychology classes devoted especially to the subject of caring for the police, Theillaumas visited the United States to obtain a victimology diploma at Washington University in 1990.

In 1996, when she was back in France, a series of suicides among the police were widely reported by the press. It was during this public relations crisis that Michel Gaudin asked her to organize the unit. Though she was the initially the sole employee of PSOU, today there are 60 psychologists working under her. The number of requests for help has risen dramatically. The unit proposes different kinds of action, which, according to madame Theillaums, are inspired by psychological research in Montreal, Canada. First there are "post-trauma actions", dedicated to those who went through a traumatic event (e.g. a mass murder, a physical wound, the suicide of a colleague). They comprise several types of reunions such as "diffusing", or "debriefings" (single-session, semi structured crisis interventions designed to reduce or prevent psychological reactions and responses to the traumatic event). Based on these debriefings, the PSOU tries to focus on monitoring the solidarity between the officers, and teaches them how to remain alert to the signs of colleagues expressing a tendency to suicide. In other words, sensors for crime are asked to play the role of sentinels for themselves.

> We try to put into play solidarity in the sense that it exists among Anglo-Saxons, that is to say that the police must remain attentive to each other, we're not asking them to take the place of psychologists, but instead to be alert to when there may be a change in behavior of a colleague after a serious personal or professional event. There are also verbally expressed messages that could help to alert others to such problems, such as, "I'm going to freak out", "If it continues like this I will jump", these are never innocuous remarks. (Theillaumas, interview 07/20/2011)

Since traumatic events are rare, the PSOU also organizes simple "conversations", which are scheduled after a phone call from a person who wants to talk about other problems that are not related to traumatic events. During these conversations, psychologists collect the complaints from the officers and help them to manage everyday stresses associated with police work. Most of the time, complaints intertwine issues spanning work and family life. Pressure to reach the objectives of the French version of COMPSTAT are seen to come into contradiction with attempts to raise kids and spend time with spouses. The primary service PSOU staff provides in these cases is to listen to the pain, and sometimes, if the officer accepts help, PSOU may attempt to mediate disputes, either within the police organization or with the family.

Recently, Eliane Theillaumas wanted to prove the importance of psychological services to reluctant policemen who might not want to admit that they might be weak or, even worse, might need outside help to deal with stress related to their professions. To this end, she decided to produce statistics about the activity of her own unit. In our terms, she would not content herself of being a sentinel: she wanted to become a sensor.

POLICE STATISTICS ARE SENSORS for social dangers such as crime and insecurity. But when the implementing organization puts pressure on them to have them capture more crime and more insecurity, sensors finds themselves in danger of gaming the numbers or falling into a psychological depression. This is why, in a reflexive turn, sentinels, such as Eterno and Silverman's sociological survey or madame Theillaumas' charts, appear to sense the dangers to which sensors are submitted. Danger is not something passive that expects to be taken into account by social forms; it apparently participates actively to the activity of the sensor. Can Tarde's prophecy of a society totally equipped with sensors integrate this reflexive dimension of the sentinels? ▪

EMMANUEL DIDIER *is a permanent researcher at the CNRS - EHESS, Groupe de sociologie politique et morale (GSPM), in Paris.*

REFERENCES

Chrystal Alec and Paul D. Mizen. 2001. "Goodhart's Law: Its Origin, Meaning and Implications for Monetary Policy," *Festschrift in honour of Charles Goodhart*, pp. 15-16 November, Bank of England.

Didier, Emmanuel. 2010. "Gabriel Tarde and Statistical Movement," in *The Social After Gabriel Tarde* M. Candea (Ed.). New York: Routledge, pp. 163-176.

Didier, Emmanuel. 2012. "L'Etat néo-libéral ment-il? "Chanstique" et statistiques de police," *Terrain*, 57, pp. 56-81.

Ehrenberg, Alain. [2000] 2010. *The Weariness of the Self: Diagnosing the History of Depression in the Contemporary Age,* Montreal: McGill-Queen's University Press.

Eterno, John A. and Eli B. Silverman. 2010. "The NYPD's Compstat : Compare Statistics or Compose Statistics." *International Journal of Police Science and Management*, 12 (3):426-449.

Hammer, Michael, James Champy. 1993. *Reengineering the Corporation. A Manifesto for Business Revolution,* New York: Harper Business.

Kelling, George and Catherine Coles. 1996. *Fixing Broken Windows: Restoring Order and Reducing Crime in Our Communities*. New York: The Free Press.

O'Connel, Paul. 2002. *An Intellectual History of the COMPSTAT Model of Police Management,* PhD Dissertation, John Jay College for Criminal Justice, City University of New York.

Osborne, David and Ted Gaebler. 1992. *Reinventing Government. How the Entrepreneurial Spirit is Transforming the Public Sector*. Reading MA:Addison-Wesley.

Tarde Gabriel. [1890] 1903. *The Laws of Imitation*. tr. Elsie Clews Parsons. New York, Henry Holt and Co.

Wilson, James. Q. 1989. *Bureaucracy. What Government Agencies Do and Why They Do It*. New York: Basic Books.

The Birds of Poyang Lake

Lyle Fearnley looks at what happens when farmers draw a line between wild and domestic that scientists miss.

The birds of Poyang Lake, do you know their number?
Flying they obscure the sun and moon
Alighting the lake-grasses are concealed.[1]

THE POYANG LAKE IN SOUTHERN CHINA is renowned for its flourishing birds. Each winter, over a million migratory waterfowl arrive from the north seeking open water and fresh grasses. One of China's first wildlife protection areas was founded on one section of the lake. Over the last three decades, however, small and medium-scale poultry farming rapidly expanded in the lake region. When fears of a global influenza pandemic grew, scientists identified Poyang Lake as a source of possible influenza emergence, fearing that transmission of viruses between wild and domestic birds could produce the next pandemic strain. Although to an anthropologist the contrast between wild and domestic suggests the classical oppositions of the raw and the cooked, of nature and culture, influenza researchers had far more urgent concerns: to make this contagious relationship into a sentinel for the pandemic.

Back in the 1960s and 1970s, Robert Webster and Kennedy Shortridge proposed that birds (and especially domestic waterfowl) could serve as sentinels for human flu pandemics. Their research transposed the temporal progression of pandemic emergence onto the categorical distinctions between species of living beings, the "frontiers of the living" (Keck 2010). An emergent influenza virus begins in wild bird reservoirs, they theorized, mutating and reassorting through domestic poultry and pigs before appearing in human populations. This suggested one could anticipate the next human pandemic by monitoring virus and disease in poultry. The emergence of a novel highly pathogenic avian influenza strain (HPAI H5N1), and the isolation of the novel virus from domestic poultry, largely confirmed this hypothesis.[2]

Shortridge had also argued that southern China was the "epicenter" of influenza viruses. The southern Chinese ecology and agriculture system entailed close contact between ducks, chickens, pigs and humans, which he believed promoted the emergence of new viruses (Shortridge and Harris 1982). When in 1997 the HPAI H5N1 strain first infected humans, global concern grew and increased funding for research followed. Scientists began to disaggregate southern China into zones of greater and lesser influenza risk, refining the location of possible sources of viral emergence. During my fieldwork in China, many researchers pointed to Poyang Lake as one such epicenter, citing scientific findings that traced the origin of internal genes from the HPAI H5N1 strain to influenza viruses isolated around Poyang and the discovery of the virus in healthy wild birds at the lake. Beginning in 2008, a group of researchers, including both international and Chinese scientists, set out to develop sentinels for influenza emergence at Poyang Lake.

Unlike Webster and Shortridge, however, they did not prioritize the detection of novel viruses. Instead, they monitored the structural conditions that produce highly pathogenic forms of the virus, a turn of attention from viral phylogeny to disease ecology. This monitoring of the ecological conditions of diseases focused on one relation in the system above all others: what they called the "wild waterfowl-domestic poultry interface" (Xiao et al. 2010). In a 2010 review article, the Poyang Lake researchers argued that a "key factor integral to the evolution of low pathogenic avian influenza into highly pathogenic avian influenza is the interaction between wild birds and poultry" (Takekawa et al. 2010). The transmission of virus across the wild-domestic interface provided opportunities for mutation and reassortment, and researchers hoped to construct a model of these interactions that would en-

---

1 A poem used as the leader in many Chinese newspaper articles about Poyang Lake and its wild bird preserve.

2 See Frédéric Keck's contribution to this issue of *LIMN*.

able the structural conditions and contact dynamics leading to viral evolution to be isolated and abstracted. These models, they claimed, could provide sentinel indications of future pandemic dangers.

Building this approach required unusual collaboration among livestock and wildlife veterinarians, ornithologists, bird migration ecologists, geographers, and economists. A set of field research projects were set up around the lake: satellite tracking of bird migrations patterns and habitat use patterns; geo-spatial mapping of rice agriculture; surveys of poultry farmers; sampling of viruses from birds; and assessments of contact rates between wild birds, poultry and humans, among other endeavors. Each research project was considered one part of an "integrated pilot study" designed to answer common questions: "where, when, and how do wild birds interface with poultry and humans?" (Xiao et al. 2010).

But what if their distinction of wild and domestic did not hold?

SCOTT NEWMAN, an American wildlife veterinarian and migration expert, stared in wonder as swan geese (*Anser cygnoides*) one by one lurched into the sky, then circled in larger and larger rings around the farmer's house. It was a damp day in the winter of 2009 and a stiff wind blew across the lake. Newman, working for the Food and Agriculture Organization on avian influenza and other zoonotic diseases, was capturing migratory birds at Poyang Lake. The birds would be surgically outfitted with transponders, then tracked by satellite when they returned north to Siberia in the spring.

But the geese he saw above him were not wild; or at least, they were bred, raised, housed, fed and sold commercially as meat by a farmer, a man surnamed Wang. Newman had found Wang's farm only that morning through what he declared to be a series of chance discoveries. First, he had been impressed by the vast number of poultry farms around Poyang Lake: Driving "from any point A to any point B," he told me in a conversation three years after his field visit, he always saw grey poultry sheds, netted ponds, and flocks of ducks or geese in the canals alongside the road. During their research, Newman and his colleagues stayed at the hotel administered by the Poyang Lake Migratory Bird Preserve in the island town of Wucheng. Over dinner, Newman began to ask the hotel staff about the poultry farms: What breeds and species of bird are being raised? Their answer surprised him: They reported species Newman did not typically see raised as domestic poultry, including swan geese.

When he visited Wang's farm, the Wang family graciously invited him for lunch, refusing to be dissuaded from their misrecognition of Newman as an American investor. Showing him the flock of swan geese hundreds strong, as well as mallard ducks, Wang proudly told Newman that bird production could easily be increased, and birds could be exported overseas. Wang also emphasized that the wildness (*yexing*) of his geese made them particularly valuable.

Newman found himself in a deeply ironic position: Wang's boasts were an influenza expert's fears. When he saw Wang's geese lift off into the sky, he thought to himself that he was looking at "what could be the link between wild and domestic birds."

"They are the perfect intermediary. Because they look identical to their conspecifics, when they are foraging, a wild bird would come right up to them, because phenotypically they are the same. But then, they go home at night, and there are other poultry around at the farm. So there's your transmission!"

NEWMAN CAME TO BELIEVE that these wild bird farms—which he soon discovered throughout the Poyang Lake region—were the key "link" in the wild bird-poultry interface. Along with colleagues, he developed a number of research projects focused on farmed wild birds: farm surveys to count the number of birds, investigations of how birds were marketed, and maps of the foraging range of the birds (Newman et al. 2012).

The integrated study at Poyang Lake began to focus on farmed wild birds as the central site of "disease implication" within the ecosystem. Although Newman and his colleagues moved to confirm their insights in new research projects, the anthropologist must examine more closely how Newman discovered the unexpected. Placing significance onto the farmed wild bird as a reified "link"—to be counted, mapped, and described—displaces attention from the practices that went into farming the wild birds in the first place. To detect the unexpected, the sentinel must cultivate an ability to question scientific objects by examining how these objects are modified by practices.

From this perspective, the distinction of wild and domestic life itself—the conceptual core of the wild bird-poultry interface—can be understood as a product of strategic practices oriented towards the future (Bourdieu 1990). It is through the labor of domestication—practices of capturing, breeding, feeding, and so on—that a qualitative difference is cultivated in the continuum of living beings, a difference of quality which becomes the precondition for categorical symbolic distinction. Moreover, the wild bird farmer approaches this distinction of wild and domestic from a reflexive position (Rabinow 1996; Descola 1996). The symbolic and material dimensions of the distinction become the *object* of practice. The goal is not domestication, *per se*, but rather the manipulation of the distinction of wild and domestic to produce new matters, new meanings, and new values.

Farmer Wang's emphasis on the value of wildness (*yexing*) in his farmed swan geese makes this symbolic strategy clear. In marketing pitches at their farm, or to visitors at their stall at the Forestry Products Expo, Wang and his son constantly promoted the wildness of their geese. In contemporary China, the consumption of wild or other unusual foods is an important strategy of status differentiation, particularly when banqueting important guests (Yang 1994; Zhan 2005). For Wang, this wildness was not defined ontologically as that which was outside of human touch. Neither was it a stable characteristic of certain individual birds or species of birds. Wildness was

a collection of qualities which could be cultivated or lost. The qualities he identified included the taste of the meat, certain secondary sex characteristics, and above all, the ability to fly. After four or five generations in captivity, Wang explained to me at his farm, the birds begin to "regress" and lose their wild character.

Therefore, techniques for cultivating wildness as a collection of qualities constitute a central part of Wang's farming practices. These include periodic capture of birds from the wild, "exogamous" breeding practices, and maintaining a reserve of birds far from the village farm, where they inhabit a more "wild" environment. On the other hand, a parallel set of techniques aim to domesticate the birds, including imprinting the birds when they are born to consider humans as "parents", and habituating

"Newman stared in wonder as swan geese (Anser cygnoides) one by one lurched into the sky ..."

the geese to regular meals at the farm.

In Wang's farming, the distinction between wild and domestic is the object of a set of strategies that reflexively manipulate the material of life in order to gain symbolic distinction. When his farmed wild geese are treated as the object of new scientific studies, the strategic art that brought the geese into being may be erased. The danger of this erasure, to put it plainly, is that there is no reason to believe that Wang (or others) will continue to farm the same things; as time moves forward, strategies will shift to maintain symbolic distinction, and change along with it the links in the wild bird-poultry interface. Moreover, scientific alerts of danger, by bringing about new monitoring regimes or biosecurity standards, may well encourage unexpected shifts in farming practice.

If raising an alarm about risk or danger must awaken actors from the routines of scientific expertise and bureaucratic inertia (Chateauraynaud and Torny 1999), the construction of scientific sentinels provides a different configuration. Neither whistleblower nor expert, a sentinel must alternate between scientific conceptualization and attending to how others modify the objects of these concepts through practice. It was only because of the concept of the wild bird-poultry interface that Scott Newman paid attention to farmed wild birds. But it was only because he attended to the practices of others—farmers in the Poyang Lake area—that he discovered the limits of his own concepts. ∎

LYLE FEARNLEY *is a Ph.D. Candidate in Medical Anthropology at University of California, Berkeley and San Francisco. His dissertation examines food safety and the veterinary vocation after China's livestock revolution.*

REFERENCES

Bourdieu, Pierre. 1990. *The Logic of Practice*. Tr. Richard Nice. Stanford: Standford University Press.

Chateauraynaud, Francis and Didier Torny. 1999. *Les sombres précurseurs: une sociologie pragmatique de l'alerte et du risque*. Paris: Editions de l'EHESS.

Descola, Phillipe. 1996. "Constructing natures: Symbolic ecology and social practice." In: Phillipe Descola and Gísli Pálsson. *Nature and Society: Anthropological Perspectives*. New York: Routledge.

Keck, Frédéric. 2010. "Une sentinelle sanitaire aux frontières du vivant," *Terrain* (2010/1)54: 27–41.

Newman, Scott, Boripat Siriaroonrat, and Xiangming Xiao. 2012. "A One-Health approach to understanding dynamics of avian influenza in Poyang Lake, China." Presentation at *EcoHealth 2012*, Kunming, China.

Rabinow, Paul. 1996. "Artificiality and enlightenment: From sociobiology to biosociality" In: *Essays on the Anthropology of Reason*. Princeton: Princeton University Press.

Shortridge, K.F. and C.H. Stuart-Harris, 1982. "An influenza epicentre" *The Lancet* 320(8302): 812–3.

Takekawa, John, Diane Prosser, Scott Newman, et al. 2010. "Victims and Vectors: Highly Pathogenic Avian Influenza H5N1 and the ecology of wild birds" *Avian Biology Research* 3(2): 1–23.

Xiao, Xiangming, Scott Newman, Tracey McCracken, and Ding Changqing, 2010. "Wild waterfowl-domestic poultry-human Interfaces: An integrated pilot study in Poyang Lake, Jiangxi, China", Presentation at *The 2nd International Workshop on Community-based Data Synthesis, Analysis and Modeling of Highly Pathogenic Avian Influenza H5N1 in Asia*.

Yang, Mayfair. 1994. *Gifts, favors and banquets: The Chinese art of social relationships*. Cornell: Cornell University Press.

Zhan, Mei. 2005. "Civet cats, fried grasshoppers, and David Beckham's pajamas: Unruly bodies after SARS." *American Anthropologist*, 107(1): 31–42.

HONG KONG AS A SENTINEL POST

WHEN BIRDS DIE OF H5N1 IN CHINA'S BORDER REGION, THE WHOLE TERRITORY OF HONG KONG IS TRANSFORMED INTO A SENTINEL POST FOR PANDEMIC FLU. FRÉDÉRIC KECK SHOWS HOW THE CITY'S NEW ROLE AFFECTS RELATIONS BETWEEN HUMANS AND BIRDS IN THIS TERRITORY.

PHOTO: DAVID ILIFF

I N 2003, AFTER HELPING TO COORDINATE a tense but ultimately successful fight against SARS, a team of University of Hong Kong microbiologists published an article entitled, "The Next Influenza Pandemic: Lessons from Hong Kong." It concluded with these words: "The studies on the ecology of influenza led in Hong Kong in the 1970s, in which Hong Kong acted as a *sentinel post* for influenza, indicated that it was possible, for the first time, to do preparedness for flu on the avian level" (Shortridge, Peiris, and Guan 2003). More than thirty five years earlier, the senior author of this paper, Kennedy Shortridge, had formulated what came to be known as the "influenza epicenter" hypothesis: Ducks and pigs living in proximity to humans in rice farming areas in South China create a perfect environment for the mutations and reassortment of flu viruses. Because SARS had caused both public health and governance crises in Hong Kong, in the following years the city made a major investment in research on emerging infectious diseases. Ken Shortridge's prophecy, formulated decades earlier in response to the 1968 flu epidemic in the region, was finally taken seriously. This essay will reflect on what it means to name a city as a sentinel post, and in particular, on the relation between humans and animals in this setting.

The first major focus of Hong Kong's expanded surveillance was the H5N1 virus, a strain of avian influenza that killed eight humans and 5000 birds in 1997. Lethal in humans, this virus appeared to be a candidate for the next great pandemic, though ultimately the difficulty of transmission between humans limited its scope (Peiris, de Jong, and Guan 2007). The 1997 outbreak showed that "preparedness" – a range of activities including stockpiling vaccines and designing simulations of a human-to-human transmission (Lakoff 2006) – should be practiced "on the avian level." Tracking the mutations and reassortments of the flu virus in birds allowed

RIGHT TOP Veterinarians take samples from ducks in a live poultry market.
RIGHT CENTER A farmer vaccinates young chicks in a poultry farm.
RIGHT BOTTOM A customer checks the health of a chicken in a live poultry market.

microbiologists to anticipate a new strain that could successfully pass between humans.

When the SARS virus arrived in Hong Kong at the beginning of 2003 after emerging on the mainland in nearby Guangzhou a couple of months earlier, the team of microbiologists led by Ken Shortridge initially believed that it was a reemergence of the H5N1 virus. The virus produced the same symptoms in humans, and appeared to have transmitted in the same way from animals. After two weeks were lost testing for H5N1, the research team applied to SARS the same techniques of description that allowed them to successfully respond to the 1997 virus. They identified SARS as

a coronavirus, and traced its animal origins in civet cats – consumed in Chinese traditional medicine – and bats. Considering animals as sentinels of emerging infectious diseases led the researchers to search for not just one but a multiplicity of viruses. As in other parts of the world, virologists in Hong Kong often describe themselves as "virus hunters" to emphasize their attentiveness to the different pathways of viruses from animals to humans.

But there is a shift from using animals as sentinels to considering a whole *territory* as a sentinel post for the emergence of viruses. A sentinel post is not only a space where sentinels are posted to watch

for signals of threats. By redrawing their territory through the pathways of viruses, Hong Kong microbiologists have trained a whole range of actors - experts, administrations, farmers, birdwatchers, and even Buddhist authorities – to express their relation to animals in the language of viruses (Keck 2010). How do all these actors fit together into a "sentinel post"? How do they configure or reconfigure relationships between humans and animals in the perspective of a coming pandemic? And how does the singularity of the territory of Hong Kong allow this transformation?

HONG KONG IS THE GATEWAY where commodities produced in China are inspected and distributed to destinations around the world. Hong Kong's ambivalent relationship to its powerful neighbor has been transmitted from colonial to postcolonial times. Hong Kong residents are at once dependent on China for their wealth and suspicious of the quality and safety of the products coming from the mainland. During the SARS outbreak, when China refused to declare its first cases to the WHO, Hong Kong took on the role of sentinel in alerting the rest of the world to this new disease. Being a border territory, like the envelope of a cell, Hong Kong has become particularly sensitive to a variety of dangers coming from China.

There is more in the notion of a "sentinel post" than simply the tracing of a gateway. Not only does the sentinel send signals of possible threats from the border, it can also be the victim of the danger it signals. The territory serves not only as a stage for actors but also as a choir for a tragedy. In 2003, Hong Kong residents, and particularly nurses, were among the first victims of SARS (Abraham 2007). In responding to the H5N1 virus threat, the Hong Kong government in 1997 decided to kill all the live poultry raised on the territory. This decision proved prescient as the reservoir for the H5N1 virus was successfully eradicated. In the context of major anxiety about the handover of the British colony to the People's Republic of China, the 1997 killing – or "culling" as it was euphemistically called – appeared as ambiguous. It showed that the new Hong Kong government cared for its human population, but also that it could act powerfully on animals to guarantee social order. A Chinese saying goes: "Kill the cock to frighten the monkey."

Since sentinels are often the first to die in the face of a new threat, can we say that they are sacrificed for the sake of those who remain? Such a statement would fail to take account of the passionate interest of those who are involved with sentinel animals, and their participation in the production of a sentinel post. Hong Kong's existence as a sentinel post was not only an alliance between experts in microbiology who focused on tracking the invisible mutation of viruses and the government which made decisions and mobilized resources to avoid the pandemic. The transformation of the territory into this new role also involved a greater number of actors and sensors. First, on the frontline are poultry farmers and retailers. After the government issued a Voluntary Surrender Act – note the military vocabulary – to close poultry farms in Hong Kong, only thirty enterprises remain today in what used to be a vibrant sector of the local economy. These farms are protected by extensive "measures of biosecurity (*shengwu anquan*)" (Hinchliffe and Bingham 2008): ponds to clean boots and wheels, fences and nets to confine the birds, etc. All chickens are vaccinated, save for a hundred "sentinels" that are meant to die first when a new virus reaches the farm. The Chinese characters used to describe these chickens, *"shaobingji,"* literally translate as "chickens that whistle like soldiers."

Live poultry cannot be bought on the farm. Instead, birds are moved through Cheung Sha Wan Central Market, where approximately ten thousands chickens arrive every day from both Hong Kong and mainland China. These live birds are sent to local retail markets, where consumers can have them killed by the merchant. It is now forbidden to bring live poultry back to one's home, as is still widely practiced on the mainland. Ironically, inspecting chicken's cloaca to see if it is fresh and healthy – a traditional act of hygienic interpretation – is now considered a risky behavior only conducted by trained microbiologists collecting samples. Every week, samples from live poultry markets are sent to the lab of Hong Kong University to undergo testing for mutations of the Avian Flu virus.

This technique of sampling to determine whether a novel virus is emerging is also applied to wild birds. Hong Kong is a major location for migratory birds on the East Australasian flyway, and more than 500 species have been observed on the territory. Shrimp ponds *(gei wai)* on the Pearl River Delta around the village of Mai Po have been transformed by the World Wildlife Fund into a biodiversity reserve. The government has sub-contracted the monitoring of birds in this reserve to the Hong Kong Birdwatching Society, an association created in 1953, and relies on Hong Kong University students to collect bird feces and check the flu viruses. Monitoring biodiversity in Mai Po provides important indicators of environmental changes in the territory.

As a result of the Avian Flu outbreak, amateur scientists working in Mai Po came into a curious interaction with religious practitioners. The Hong Kong government had decided to close Mai Po reserve for three weeks every time a bird within a three kilometers perimeter of the reserve was found with H5N1. If infected birds were to be found in the urban area of Shenzhen or in the remaining poultry farms in Yuen Long, Mai Po would be shut to birdwatchers, even if no birds were infected in the reserve. To denounce what they saw as a policy lacking scientific grounding, birdwatchers joined up with Hong Kong University microbiologists to hold a press conference. They showed maps where known occurrences of H5N1 in Hong Kong converged around the most populous area of the New Territories: Mong Kok Bird Market. This is a major place for trade in wild birds, and a site for the Buddhist practice of "animal release" *(fangsheng)*. Small birds, sometimes carrying H5N1, are brought to the market in stressful conditions and released in adjacent parks. After discussions with birdwatchers, microbiologists and government administrators, the Buddhist association banned this practice in Hong Kong, and advised worshippers to release seafood rather than birds. Posters on Buddhist temples show recently freed birds turning into skeletons as they leave the island –a Buddhist-inflected depiction of birds as sentinels.

This forum on bird release serves as one example of how Hong Kong as a sentinel post has become a stage for various types of performances. Clearly all actors don't perceive the birds in the same way:

Farmers see them as commodities in a food chain, birdwatchers as species in an ecosystem, Buddhists as souls in a cycle of reincarnations. But they have learned to express their various perceptions in a common language, that of microbiology. If an Avian Flu outbreak produces tensions in local residents' ordinary perception of birds, shifting winged animals that once appeared as beneficial to eat or to watch into dangerous beings, the building of a sentinel post transforms this tension into a productive interaction. Because birds are mobile and diverse, they can sound alarms on future threats affecting humans: Trapped in the sentinel post, blurring the distinction between wild and domestic, they constitute a new kind of collective being, where relations between humans and animals are reconfigured in the language of viruses. The sentinel post is not a lonely soldier waiting for an invisible enemy: It is a choir of *personae* expressing the tensions of life on a border – between species and between countries. ∎

FRÉDÉRIC KECK *is a researcher at the CNRS and a member of the Laboratoire d'anthropologie sociale in Paris.*

REFERENCES

Abraham, Thomas. 2007. *Twenty-First Century Plague. The Story of* SARS, *with a new Preface on Avian Flu*, Hong Kong, Hong Kong University Press.

Hinchliffe, Stephen and Nick Bingham. 2008. "Mapping the multiplicities of biosecurity", in Lakoff, Andrew and Stephen Collier. 2008. (eds.) *Biosecurity Interventions. Global Health and Security in Question*, New York, SSRC-University of Columbia Press, pp. 173-193

Keck, Frédéric. 2010. *Un monde grippé*, Paris, Flammarion.

Lakoff, Andrew. 2006. "Preparing for the next Emergency", *Public Culture*, 19(2):247-271.

Peiris, Malik, Menno de Jong, and Guan Yi. 2007. "Avian Influenza Virus (H5N1): a Threat to Human Health", *Clinical Microbiology Review*, 20(2):243-267.

Shortridge, Kennedy, Malik Peiris and Yi Guan. 2003. "The Next Influenza Pandemic : Lessons from Hong Kong", *Journal of Applied Microbiology*, 94(s1):70-79.

A DEARTH OF NUMBERS

THE ACTUARY AND THE SENTINEL IN GLOBAL PUBLIC HEALTH

How do experts respond to a threat whose probability cannot be calculated but whose consequences could be catastrophic? **ANDREW LAKOFF** explores the political dynamics of sentinel devices in the case of the 2009 swine flu pandemic.

IN THE FIRST HALF OF THE NINETEENTH CENTURY, EUROPEAN GOVERNMENTS BEGAN TO gather and publish vast amounts of statistical data on the vital characteristics of populations: their rates of marriage, birth, death and disease.[1] The analysis of this data revealed that while the future was contingent, there were nonetheless certain regularities according to which governments could rationally plan. An example is the biometer, developed in the 1840s by William Farr, head of the British General Register Office. This device demonstrated the likelihood of mortality in any given year for a particular age group. It combined national census data and parish death registers to track a group of infants of the same age through life, recording the numbers still alive at periodic intervals until all had died. Such data could reveal "laws of vitality" that would make it possible to anticipate the future fate of these infants. As Farr explained: "Although we know little the labors, the privations, the happiness, the calms or tempests, which are prepared for the next generation of Europeans, we entertain little doubt that about 9000 of them will be found alive at the distant Census in 1921."[2]

This style of reasoning about disease and death can be termed *actuarial*. Like insurance, it requires historical data about patterns of incidents of events in order to make rational calculations about future probabilities. In the field of public health, however, it is applied with a different aim: to optimize the health of populations. Once there is sufficient data on differential risk of disease, it becomes possible to develop targeted interventions to reduce mortality rates. This actuarial logic serve to legitimate political decisions on risk, whether or not the potential hazard eventually appears.[3] Over time, this mode of calculation guided policy decisions in fields ranging from public health to industrial accidents to retirement pensions.

The actuarial style of reasoning, oriented toward disease prevention through the management of risk, has remained predominant among experts in public health. However, beginning in the last decades of the twentieth century it has increasingly coexisted with a different approach, one that emphasizes vigilant monitoring of the onset of an unpredictable but potentially catastrophic event. If risk management involves the creation of a common space of calculation through which planners can anticipate the likelihood of future events, vigilance assumes that the future cannot be known and that one must therefore plan for the unexpected. Rather than relying on a calculus of cost and benefit, vigilance enjoins intervention in a precautionary mode: one must act now or one may be held accountable later for the results of inaction.[4]

Two kinds of security mechanism are in play. If risk management leads to the invention of actuarial devices that assemble patterns of historical incidence, vigilance requires sentinel devices that can provide early warning of encroaching danger. An actuarial device is invented for a world in which the possible threats to collective life can be known through statistical analysis and the problem is

---

1   Ian Hacking calls this "the avalanche of printed numbers" (Hacking 1989).
2   Cited in Eyler (1979:73).

3   As Niklas Luhmann (1998: 70) writes, "the present can calculate a future that can always turn out otherwise; so the present can assure itself that it calculated correctly, even if things turn out otherwise."
4   As Francis Chateauraynaud and Didier Torny write, "It is no longer possible to say, without exposing oneself to criticism, that 'according to the calculations, the risk is negligible" (Chateauraynaud and Torny 2005:4).

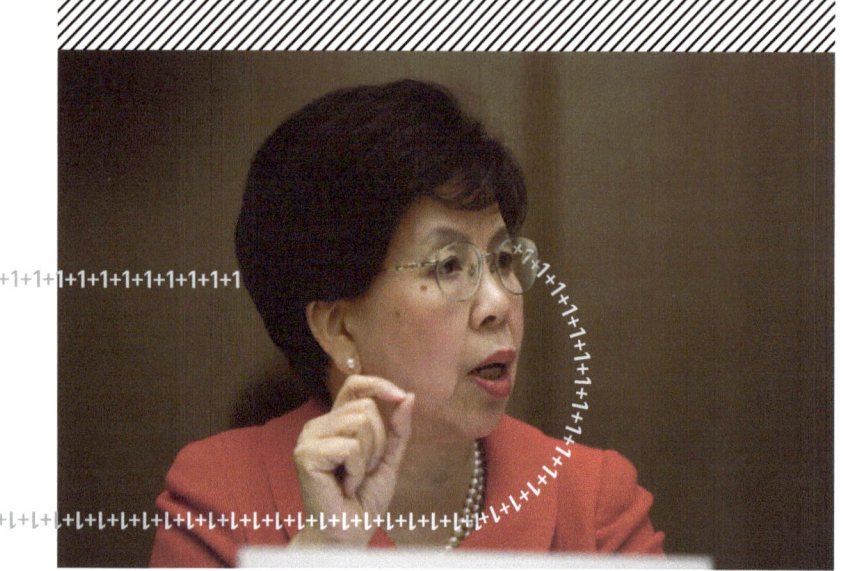

DR. MARGARET CHAN Director-General of the World Health Organization.

one of accumulating enough data to guide cost-effective intervention. A sentinel device, in contrast, is devised in order to stimulate action when decision is imperative but knowledge is incomplete.

Sentinel devices are especially salient for experts in monitoring threats whose onset may be sudden and unpredictable, and whose initial effects may be imperceptible to humans. In the field of public health, such tools are designed to detect the emergence of unexpected or unknown disease. One example of vigilant monitoring for encroaching pathogens comes from "viral forecasting," such as a Google-funded enterprise that collects and tests samples of African bush meat for the emergence of zoonotic disease based on the premise that such a system can "stop the next pandemic before it starts" (see Lachenal forthcoming). Another is "syndromic disease surveillance," which aims to detect signals of a new epidemic even before doctors have made any diagnoses, for instance by looking at anomalies in emergency room visits or in the use of over-the-counter medications (see Fearnley).

While these devices are designed to alert officials to a significant event in the present, they provide little information about what is likely to happen next. For this reason they are typically linked to guidelines or protocols for taking authorized action in the face of uncertainty. Thus sentinel devices do not operate autonomously, but are integrated into systems of alert-and-response, including preparedness plans that structure official response and decision instruments that guide intervention upon the onset of an event. Such responses, however, may be subject to criticism from actors who are invested in an actuarial approach and who are suspicious of vigilance as a technocratic mode. A recent European controversy around vaccination policy—though it played out in an "ethical" idiom—can be understood as a critique, from some quarters of public health, of the legitimacy of the sentinel device as a guide to techno-political intervention.

THE NEXT PANDEMIC

When the newly reasserted influenza virus A/H1N1 made its appearance among humans in the Spring 2009, it seemed at first to be the pathogen the international health community had been preparing for. Dozens had apparently died in Mexico from a respiratory ailment, and hundreds more were hospitalized. Reports of cases from around the United States indicated rapid transmission of the virus. There was a possibility that this would become a deadly pandemic, but its key statistical characteristics—in particular, its case fatality ratio—were not yet known. Within weeks an extensive public health apparatus had taken hold of the virus, tracking its global extension through reference laboratories, mapping its genomic sequence, collating data on hospitalization and death rates, working to distribute anti-viral medicines and develop a vaccine, and communicating risk to various publics. While some elements of this apparatus were decades old, such as the Global Influenza Surveillance Network and the egg-based technique of vaccine production—others were quite new, such as internet-based outbreak reporting systems, molecular surveillance, and national pandemic preparedness plans.

Based on reports from Mexico and the US, WHO Director-General Margaret Chan declared a Public Health Emergency of International Concern (PHEIC) under the newly revised International Health Regulations (IHR). Here the sentinel was linked up to a decision instrument designed to guide political-administrative action. Following IHR protocol, Chan appointed an Emergency Committee constituted of recognized influenza experts, who recommended a Phase Four Pandemic Alert. Given the controversy that followed, it is important to point out that the definition of "pandemic" from WHO's 2009 preparedness guidance document referred to "sustained community-level outbreaks" in multiple regions but made no reference to the severity of the virus.

Four days later, on April 29, the Emergency Committee voted to raise the pandemic alert level to Phase Five, indicating that national health authorities should move from "preparedness" to "response" activities. Chan assured the public that WHO was tracking the emerging pandemic across multiple registers—clinical, epidemiological, and viral—and advised national health ministers to "immediately activate their pandemic plans" (Chan 2009a). For North American and European governments, among other things this meant triggering advanced purchase agreements with vaccine manufacturers to produce millions of doses in time for anticipated fall immunization campaigns. In the absence of epidemiological data on the severity of the virus, the pandemic alert system alongside national preparedness plans provided government officials with guideposts for action.[5]

On June 11, Chan announced pandemic alert Phase Six, a full global pandemic. In her public statement, she pointed to the agency's vigilance as the event unfolded: "No previous pandemic has been detected so early or watched so closely, in real-time, right at the very beginning. The world can now reap the benefits of investments, over the past five years, in pandemic preparedness" (Chan 2009b). At the same time, she also warned of ongoing uncertainty: "The virus writes the rules and this one, like all influenza viruses, can change the rules, without rhyme or reason, at any time." Vigilant watchfulness would continue to be necessary.

As of early July, experts were still trying to figure out what H1N1's "rules" were, in particular its rules of transmissibility and virulence. A critical problem remained the lack of data on the overall incidence, as opposed to the number of fatalities, of H1N1 in the exposed population. This was the well-known "problem of the denominator." A team of epidemiologists argued for immediate investment in serologic surveys so that the case fatality ratio could be calculated: "Without good incidence estimates," they wrote, "estimates of severity will continue to suffer from an unknown denominator. The effectiveness of control measures will be difficult to assess without accurate measures of local incidence" (Lipsitch et al. 2009). This was an attempt to move from vigilance to risk management through the intensive gathering, sharing and analysis of epidemiological data. The Director of the US Institute of Medicine described such efforts as "epidemic science in real time," through which "scientists can enable policies to be adjusted appropriately as an epidemic scenario unfolds" (Fineberg and Wilson 2009).

Significant political and economic decisions had to be made in the absence of fully elaborated data on risk. Beginning in the summer 2009, the US government spent $1.6 billion on 229 million doses of vaccine in what the *Washington Post* later called "the most ambitious immunization campaign in US history" (Stein 2010). In the early fall, unanticipated delays in vaccine production combined with high demand led to criticism of health officials for poor planning, which faded as the anticipated wave of H1N1 arrived without causing a catastrophic number of deaths.

In Europe, when the fall wave arrived, the apparent mildness of the virus led to widespread public skepticism about state-led vaccination campaigns. The French government spent an estimated five hundred million euros on a campaign that in the end immunized only ten percent of the population. By the winter, the governments of France, Germany and England all sought to renegotiate their advanced purchase agreements with vaccine manufactures

and to unload their excess doses on poor countries in the Global South at bargain prices.

A series of political controversies then erupted over the intensive public health response to H1N1. In *Le Monde*, former French Red Cross president Marc Gentilini admonished the government for its spending on the campaign, noting that "preparing for the worst wasn't necessarily preparing correctly" (Chaon 2010). A physician and legislator for the governing conservative party decried the misallocation of public health resources, saying "the cost is more than the deficit of all France's hospitals and is three times [the amount spent] on cancer care" (Daneshkhu and Jack 2010). The French government defended its actions on the grounds of precaution: "I will always prefer to be too prudent than not enough," said President Sarkozy (Whalen and Gauthier-Villars 2010).

The attention of critics then turned to the warnings from international flu specialists that had led to the mass vaccination campaigns. As Gentilini put it, "I don't blame the health minister, but the medical experts. They created an apocalyptic scenario. There was pressure from the World Health Organization, which began waving the red warning flags too early" ("Flu Vaccine" 2010). The head of the French Socialist Party demanded a parliamentary inquiry, calling the vaccination campaign a "fiasco" and arguing that multinational drug companies were "the big winners in this affair" (Daneshkhu and Jack, 2010). The Chair of the Council of Europe's Health Committee, a German physician, convoked public hearings on the matter, charging that the WHO pandemic declaration was "one of the greatest medical scandals of the century" (Macrae 2010).

Witnesses before the European Council's Health Committee argued that scarce health resources had been squandered on a virus that turned out to be less dangerous than seasonal flu, and that such resources should have been spent on "real" killers, whether heart disease in wealthy countries or infant diarrhea in poor ones. A German epidemiologist cited annual mortality statistics to criticize the WHO's emphasis on managing potential outbreaks at the expense of treating the actual "great killers" whose toll was attested to by epidemiological data: "I would like to point out that of the 827,155 deaths in 2007 in Germany about 359,000 come from cardiovascular diseases, about 217,000 from cancer, 4968 from traffic accidents, 461 from HIV/AIDS and zero from SARS or Avian Flu" (Keil 2010). Here, coming from one segment of public health experts, we find the public display of numbers used to make the case that rational intervention must be based on risk calculation rather than on precaution against potential catastrophe.

But rather than see the WHO as engaged in a different type of reasoned action, critics denounced a lack of objectivity, arguing that conflicts of interest among members

---

5   The WHO preparedness guidance explained the function of the alert system as follows: "This phased approach is intended to help countries and other stakeholders to anticipate when certain situations will require decisions and decide at which point main actions should be implemented" (World Health Organization 2009).

FIGURE 1:
Statistician William
Farr's diagram
of the relation
between elevation
and cholera risk,
based on data from
the 1848 London
epidemic

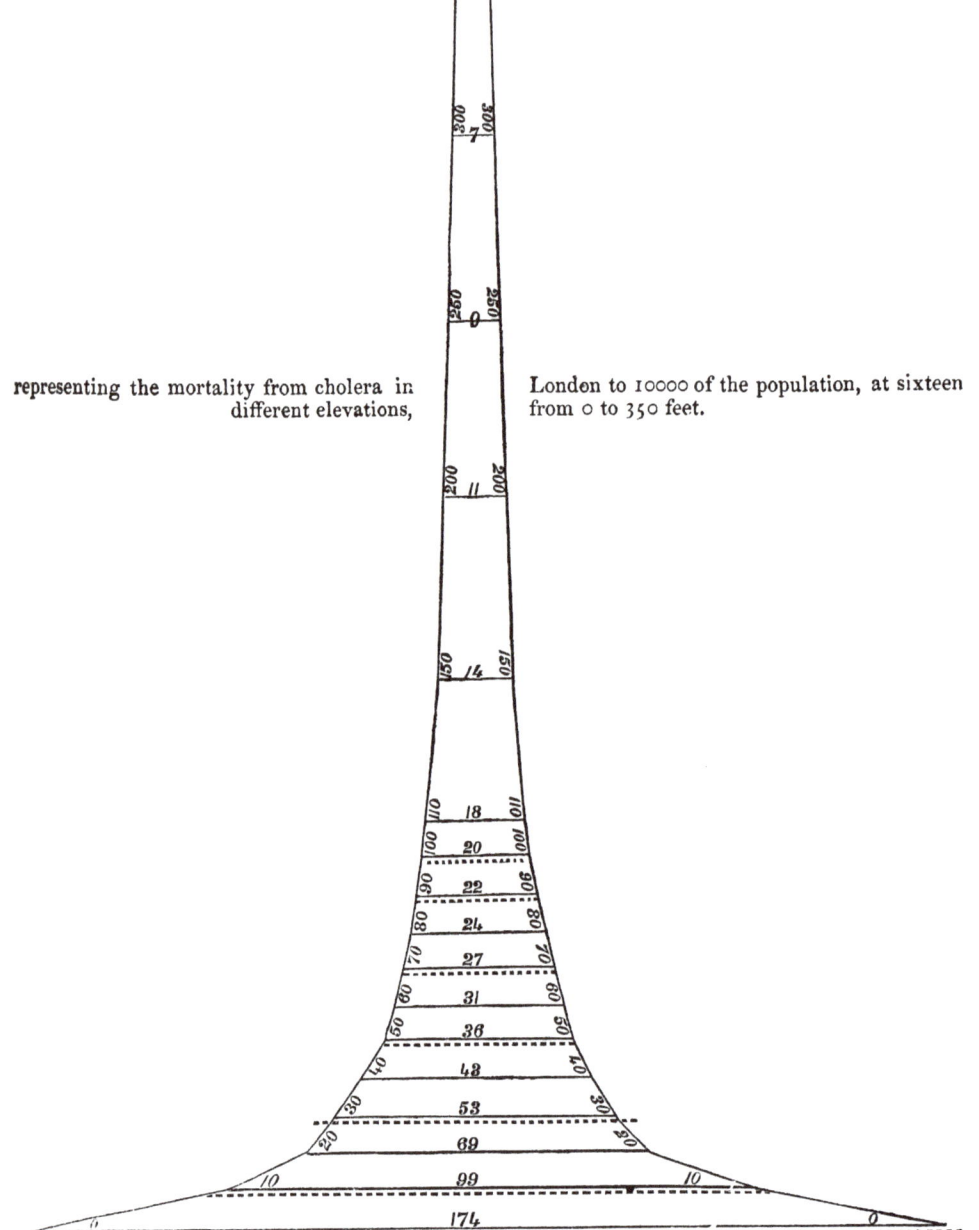

representing the mortality from cholera in different elevations, London to 10000 of the population, at sixteen from 0 to 350 feet.

The figures in the centre express the number of deaths from cholera to 10000 inhabitants living' at the elevations expressed in feet on the sides of the diagram.

The length of the *black horizontal lines* shows the *calculated* relative fatality of cholera in districts at relative elevations indicated by the height from the base of the diagram. The *dotted lines* indicate the mean mortality *observed* in the elevations given. Thus :—in districts at 90 feet above the Thames, the average mortality from cholera was 22 in 10000 inhabitants.

1+1+1+1+1+1+1+1+1+1+1+1+1+1+1+1+1+1+1+1+1+1+1+1+1+1+1+1+1+1+1+1+1+1+1+1+1+1+1+1+1+1+1+1+1+1+1+1+1+1+1

of the Emergency Committee must have led to the pandemic declaration. One source of suspicion was the removal of the measurement of severity from the WHO preparedness guidance document several months before the appearance of H1N1. In June, an investigative report in the *British Medical Journal* revealed paid consulting relations between leading influenza experts and vaccine manufacturers (Cohen and Carter 2010). The same week, the Council of Europe released its report, concluding that the pandemic declaration had led to "a distortion of priorities of public health services across Europe, waste of huge sums of public money, [and the] provocation of unjustified fears among Europeans," and suggesting that WHO deliberations had been tainted by unstated conflicts of interest between experts and the drug companies that profited from the vaccine campaign (Parliamentary Assembly 2010).

In response to these allegations, Chan chartered a review of the agency's response under the aegis of IHR. The Review Committee's final report, released in May 2011, absolved the WHO influenza experts of overstating the seriousness of the pandemic. "Reasonable criticism can be based only on what was known at the time and not on what was later learnt," the Committee argued, pointing out that "the degree of severity of the pandemic was very uncertain throughout the middle months of 2009, well past the time, for example, when countries would have needed to place orders for vaccine" (World Health Organization 2011). In the case of a novel pathogen, the virulence of an encroaching pandemic cannot be determined based on accumulated knowledge about the past. At a moment of critical decision, one will inevitably suffer from a dearth of numbers.

In the 1840s, the actuarial device in public health was invented in the context of an attempt to know and manage the regularities of collective life. A century and a half later, sentinel devices proliferated in response to a different problem, that of the unpredictable but potentially catastrophic outbreak in a globally interconnected world. These two approaches to securing public health encountered one another around the question of what kind of event H1N1 was to be: an alarm precipitously sounded or a bullet barely dodged. ∎

ANDREW LAKOFF *teaches sociology, anthropology and communication at the University of Southern California.*

REFERENCES

Chan, Margaret. 2009a. "Statement by WHO Director-General, Dr Margaret Chan", 29 April. Available at: http://www.who.int/mediacentre/news/statements/2009/h1n1_20090429/en/index.html.

Chan, Margaret. 2009b. "Statement to the press by WHO Director-General Dr Margaret Chan." 11 June. URL: http://www.who.int/mediacentre/news/statements/2009/h1n1_pandemic_phase6_20090611/en/index.html

Chaon, Anne. 2010. "France joins Europe flu vaccine sell-off," *Agence France-Presse,* January 3.

Chateauraynaud, Francis and Didier Torny. 2005. "Mobiliser autour d'un risque. Des lanceurs aux porteurs d'alerte" in *Risques et crises alimentaires,* Cécile Lahellec (ed.), Lavoisier, pp. 329–339.

Cohen, Deborah and Phillip Carter. 2010. "WHO and the Pandemic Flu 'Conspiracies," *British Medical Journal,* 340(c2912):1274–1279.

Daneshkhu, Scheherazade and Andrew Jack. 2010. "Sarkozy under fire on flu vaccine 'fiasco'." *Financial Times,* January 5.

Eyler, John. 1979. *Victorian Social Medicine: The Ideas and Methods of William Farr.* Baltimore: Johns Hopkins University Press.

Fearnley, Lyle. 2008. "Redesigning Syndromic Surveillance for Biosecurity," in A. Lakoff and S. Collier, *Biosecurity Interventions: Global Health and Security in Question.* New York: Columbia University Press, pp. 61–88.

Fineberg, Harvey V., and Mary Elizabeth Wilson. 2009. "Epidemic science in real time." *Science* 324(5920):987.

"Flu Vaccine Overstock." 2010. *PRI's The World.* January 11, URL: http://www.theworld.org/2010/01/flu-vaccine-overstock/

Hacking, Ian. 1989. *The Taming of Chance.* Cambridge, U.K.: Cambridge University Press.

Keil, Ulrich. 2010. "Introductory statement by Prof. Dr. Ulrich Keil," Social, Health and Family Affairs Committee of the Parliamentary Assembly of the Council of Europe. Hearing on "The handling of the H1N1 pandemic: more transparency needed?" Strasbourg, 26 January.

Lachenal, Guillaume. Forthcoming. "Lessons in medical nihilism. Virus hunters, neoliberalism and the AIDS crisis in Cameroon", in Wenzel Geissler ed., *Science and the Parastate in Africa,* Durham: Duke University Press.

Lipsitch, Marc, Steven Riley, Simon Cauchemez, et al. 2009. "Managing and reducing uncertainty in an emerging influenza pandemic." *New England Journal of Medicine,* 361(2):112–115.

Luhmann, Niklas. 1998. "Describing the Future," in *Observations on Modernity.* Stanford: Stanford University Press.

Macrae, Fiona. 2010. "The 'false' pandemic: Drug firms cashed in on scare over swine flu, claims Euro health chief." *Daily Mail,* January 17.

Parliamentary Assembly. 2010. "Handling of the H1N1 pandemic: more transparency needed." *Resolution 1749(1).*

Stein, Rob. 2010. "Millions of H1N1 vaccine doses may have to be discarded," *Washington Post,* Thursday, April 1.

Whalen, Jeanne and David Gauthier-Villars. 2010. "European Governments Cancel Vaccine Orders," *Wall Street Journal,* January 10.

World Health Organization. 2009. Global Influenza Programme. *Pandemic influenza preparedness and response: a WHO guidance document.* World Health Organization.

World Health Organization. 2011. "Implementation of the International Health Regulations (2005)." Report of the review committee on the functioning of the International Health Regulations (2005) in relation to pandemic (H1N1) 2009. Geneva: WHO. 5 May 2011. *64th World Health Assembly:* 17.

the apocalypse and the crazy farm scenario

The Large Hadron Collider in Switzerland has to be constantly monitored to detect possible effects of radiation. **Sophie Houdart** describes a machine designed to capture every potential sign of threat.

In a book entitled *The Large Hadron Collider. Unraveling the Mysteries of the Universe*, Martin Beech, physician and professor of astronomy, starts his depiction of "Europe's exultant shrine to nuclear physics", the CERN (the European Organisation for Nuclear research), as follows: "For over 20 years now, if you listened very carefully, the ground below the verdant fields of the *Pays de Gex* region of France has trembled very slightly and perhaps, just perhaps, faintly hummed"(Beech 2010, 41). In this in-between scientific zone, half in France, half in Switzerland, *something* apparently calls for a fabulous destiny. Most of the literature on the LHC (Large Hadron Collider) inevitably opens with the quasi-same rhetoric. As the biggest experimental device in the world, the LHC is a machine that accumulates superlatives: 100 meters under the ground, particles are accelerated to 99.9999991% of the speed of light, execute some 11245 rotations around the loop and collide one with each other about 600 million times per second ... The incredible complexity supporting these records has been designed for an even more incredible aim: to provide "a journey inside the deepest structure of matter", to discover "the fundamental laws that determine the behavior of nature", to understand "the first principles that govern the universe" (Guidice 2010, 3), and to provide "insights into the origin of the universes"(Beech 2010, vii). Respect. Admiration. Adoration, even.

The question remains how such a peculiar site (the Pays de Gex and CERN, headquartered there) and the unraveling of cosmos's mysteries are connected. How to *commensurate* one with the other?

APOCALYPTIC SCENARIO FOR BIG MACHINE

In March 2007, a complaint was filed against CERN by Louis Sancho and Walter L. Wagner (court case 1:2008cv00136), who had just created the association *Citizens Against The Large Hadron Collider* and wanted to pre-empt the LHC's launch by demanding its postponement. As reported by Martin Beech, "the plaintiffs were not especially worried about the health and safety of the CERN engineers and researchers. Rather, and in some highly laudable sense, the plaintiffs were concerned about the potential death of all of humanity, an Earth-crushing 6.8 billion people, as well as the destruction of earth itself". October 1st 2008. The case

was closed and the complaint rejected under the motive that the suit revolved around a debate too "complex" that was beyond its jurisdiction but was "of concern to the whole world"[1]. On the side of the physicists, the case was resolved in the statement that "our safety is assured by the fact that the world is already 4.5 billion years old – indeed, the very existence of the Sun, Moon, planets, and stars are glittering testaments to the safety of the LHC. Nature has already run nearly half a million experiments, similar to that which will be conducted at the LHC during the next decade, in our upper atmosphere, and Earth, philosophical quibbling aside, is still here and we are still very much alive (50)." The astronomical objects are taken as proof – as valuable witnesses – that the LHC cannot harm us.

The conclusion that we can draw from such an argument is that the LHC is on Nature's side. By extension, this position alone provides proof for its own innocence and simultaneously disarms the question of responsibility. The situation on which the controversy is based is interesting: It is not the experimenting performed within that provides information on what happens on the outside (the state of the world, the mysteries of the cosmos), but the state of the world itself (the fact that the world still exists as we speak) that provides information on what is going on within – and, in this instance, also guarantees that what is going on is not likely to put us in danger.

MONITORING

While it is up to the theorists to vouch for the impossibility of a black hole that will swallow us all up, it is only specialists in our very immediate surroundings who are qualified to assess the LHC's *realistic* effects on the world. Sonja Kleiner heads the "Environment" Department. From the outset, she gives me a very detailed description of the perimeters of her department. The section managed by Sonja is in charge of measuring radiation and protecting the environment. Radiology has, of course, existed as a practice area since CERN was set up, but over the last decade, this aspect of CERN's work has had to be rebalanced with the "protec-

---

1 "The United States Defendants move for dismissal for lack of subject matter jurisdiction or for summary judgment on other grounds" (Order 2008).

tion" side and the various environmental aspects connected with standard industrial equipment. "We carry out environmental monitoring. We are responsible for carrying out a measuring programme that we take to the authorities and host countries." The Environment Department covers eleven areas: water, air, soils, ionizing and non-ionizing radiation, dangerous substances, waste, energy, noise, natural environment protection and the prevention of environmental incidents. A hundred or so measuring and sampling stations are spread out over the entire zone defined by the LHC loop, but "we still want to refine our *surveillance net,*" specifies Sonja.

A few days after my first visit, I meet up with Julien in the "Environment" Department for "Wednesday's routine". It's 8 o'clock in the morning. I accompany Julien as he collects a series of readings taken every fortnight. "All the elements we're going to look at have a lifespan," Julien begins. This is why other samples are taken (especially from rivers) at longer intervals (once a month). We set out on our circuit at Station 910 where are recuperated the waste of the entire LHC loop used to cool the gigantic LHC installation. 230 cubic meters of cooling water are discharged here. In the "station", the small pre-fab building behind us, Julien carries out "conventional measurings" of temperature, pH, water muddying and conductivity. An amount of water is continually automatically taken as a sample. "Everything on the site is found here. For example, if a truck arrives with chemical products and there's a leak, or a tank that freezes and bursts, or a handling error, whatever scenario, anything that spills will drain if it rains or there's a storm, and it'll spread the pollution. We have to be able to collect all the different water and measure it all." The work would be less tricky if the measurements did not *also* change according to the vagaries of the weather. "The measures all change if it's raining but also, and above all, (and it's very important in terms of measuring) if it snows, and the villages salt the roads. We find the salt in our measurements!" The monitoring stations allow them to record an "electrocardiogram" of the LHC (what it inhales, what it exhales), on which the sounds of the world are *recorded* – snowfall and salting but also, as we shall see, disasters that occur on the other side of the world. "In general, that's why we take these measurements. If a tank is leaking, we have to be capable of measuring it", muses Julien. Almost as an aside, he adds that, on request, the staff at the Environment Department sometimes carry out readings on a higher frequency, even "every day... for example, if something happens on the other side of the world... Fukushima is measured... but that's not official. The IRSN [the french Institute for Radiation Protection and Nuclear Safety] took measurements, but they weren't the only ones..." These filters, like all the others he collects, are analyzed in CERN's laboratory as well as by another Swiss organization. Nothing disappears and everything is transformed, Julien says on several occasions, like a litany.

We reach another station and enter the building. This time, we take a sample of from each of the station's two ventilation shafts. The LHC requires two ventilation units because it is circular and air must be drawn in from both sides. "We take a sample of each ventilation. We measure the aerosols, very fine dust in suspension in the air." We move on to the next stations, one after the other. Each station records very different aspects. One of them collects 30,000 cubic meters per hour, another only 2,000. "We don't want to use statistics to establish significance because we're talking about very small figures. We have to be able to take into consideration things that might appear negligible." We return to the car, leaving the main road to set off along a track that takes us through planted fields. Julien points out a field of asparagus on my right where they take samples every year.

We return to the "Environment" Department and unload the car. All the samples we have brought back are distributed right away. A thick binder of forms that Julien had spent much of the day filling with (type of measurements) go to Fabrice, the plastic drums and glass bottles go to Martine, who also archives the filters.

In order for it to play its role to the full, this sentinel has a *topography*. It's the zone defined by the LHC loop that constitutes it. Inside the loop, everything, or almost everything, is enlisted in the monitoring system. Acting like surveillance towers, the stations allow us to "see" a great number of things: ventilation that comes in and comes out, but also atmospheric changes that occur here and there on our planet. Here, it is to the air and its properties, amongst other things, that we owe this potential of vision.

A CRAZY FARM SCENARIO

Back from collecting air, and also water and soil samples, I sit down at the table with Fabrice from the Environment Department, to study a map of the region that delineates the boundaries of LHC. All around us are measuring instruments, vats, pipettes and flasks. We are in the Department's analysis laboratory. "We take the worst scenario. We do our calculations with the worst nuclide, phosphorus-32. We imagine that it's passed into the air and entered into the cows' milk that will be given to children, for example. It's kind of the German way of seeing things, and we call it the "Crazy Farm Scenario", which consists of always imagining a child who's wallowing in the mud and drinking stagnant water, and breathing the air in the same place without ever moving from there. Another version, on the contrary, consists of determining realistic lifestyles. We'll imagine that people grow their own food, but really, realistically, it's quite hard to produce 15% of it yourself! Here, we adopt a fairly realistic model, but we still take into account the worst nuclide... We imagine a field and say that it might have cows in it, for example." These scenarios are used to size up the monitoring installations. "We really do measure what people breathe. And we've never found anything - totally insignificant amounts. Except for once; one measurement above the natural value, and the physicist was very pleased because it validated his model. And even then, the measurement in itself was negligible. So we continue to measure nothing".

Having to adapt to the shifting legislative environment in Europe (which has recently included new protocols related to the Euratom Directive), staff members at LHC have now to consider laws far stricter with regard to vegetation and animals. As Fabrice explained, "We're going to have to keep at it and look at the impact on the mosses themselves. Now we'll have to concern ourselves with moss, cows and trees...I ask myself how far it will go!"

Alongside the many and unexpected connections it establishes, the LHC seems to endeavor to *disconnect* a certain number of things. What staff members at CERN refuse to connect is the LHC and industrial pollution, or the LHC and the demise of the Earth. In order to convince people outside of CERN of these disconnections, measurements have to be refined to the point where they "measure nothing", or

make the micro black holes into the perfectly inoffensive avatars of cosmological black holes. One needs to remind himself or herself continually that scale counts, and that all the superlatives duly employed to describe what goes on at CERN should not lead to confusion: In spite of the colossal aspect of the machine, it is the infinitely small and the infinitely nothing that it describes. The operations through which this scale of work continues to be connected to the world, to humankind and to the universe become crucial: homogeneization, stabilization, simulation, synchronization, correlation, alignment, miniature reproduction and so on.

As a potential site of the drama, the LHC is subject to extremely close scrutiny, extremely careful measures. By equipping itself to tirelessly document the miniscule, the LHC picks up more of the noise of the world than it needs. From being a place vulnerable to a big disaster, it becomes a place through which danger becomes perceptible in its smallest aspects - of whatever nature that danger may be. ■

SOPHIE HOUDART *is an anthropologist of science, member of the Centre for Ethnology and Comparative Sociology (LESC), CNRS, France. Her research deals with contemporary Japan and the notion of scale in the production of knowledge.*

Translated by Lucy Lyall-Grant

REFERENCES
Beech, Martin. 2010. *The Large Hadron Collider. Unraveling the Mysteries of the Universe.* London: Springer Science and Business Media.
Giudice, Gian Francesco. 2010. *A Zeptospace Odyssey. A Journey into the Physics of the LHC.* Oxford: Oxford University Press.
Order Granting Federal Defendants' Motion to Dismiss. Signed by Judge Helen Gillmor on September 26, 2008.

THE ORIGINS OF EXTINCTION

What do barn swallows reveal about the future? In the biogeographical space of "the Zone" around Chernobyl, **Adriana Petryna** shows us how they force us to think about the origins of extinction.

Is it an ecological wonderland or a post-industrial wasteland? Ever since the 1986 Chernobyl nuclear disaster in Ukraine, scores of researchers have come to the so-called Zone, an area 30 kilometers in diameter circumscribing the disaster site, to explore how the world's worst accidental nuclear release affected flora and fauna. Abandoned and stripped of human activities, the Zone has become a site of heated debate about the long-term effects of radiochemical exposures. A team of researchers based in Texas focusing mainly on bank voles found no evidence of negative biological effects "even among fauna that experienced chronic exposure to the highest levels" of radiation (Baker and Wickliffe 2011). A particularly contaminated area near Glyboke Lake "was always a joy to visit" given the alleged abundance of large mammals such as wild boar, moose, wolves, and roe deer. This team concluded that "it was the presence or absence of humans—not radiation—that influenced the abundance" of certain mammals. Like the pieces of a sliding puzzle, animals (and humans) abandon, move into, or reoccupy ecological niches. The end-configurations of these range shifts are *"as expected based on local ecology."*

The long-term assessment of another team of researchers, however, turns this horizon of expected ends on its head. The sightings of large mammals in the Zone, biologists Timothy Mousseau and Anders Møller argue, are anecdotal and the fanfare over those sightings obscures the real chaos taking place a few notches down the animal kingdom, where the long-term presence of radiation simulates, in some respects, what the "hour" of extinction might look like for certain

birds and small mammals. They write, "The best-studied group, birds, shows a 50 percent decrease in species richness and a 66 percent drop in abundance in the most contaminated areas compared to areas with normal background radiation in the same neighborhood" (2011:38). In areas of moderate to high contamination, Mousseau and Møller report dramatically higher mutation rates and developmental abnormalities and lower rates of survival and fertility (ibid.). Radiation is causing not only unusual tumors in the beaks of barn swallows and wing discoloration, but also, by dint of those and other physiological impacts, radiation acts as a kind of bio-ecological solvent in which the recruitment of potential mates is compromised, reproduction rates decline, species go missing, and animal die-offs take place.

These findings raise questions about the very nature of extinction, or of how certain parameters of its recognition strategically coalesce in particular times and places under threat. Recognition is a strong meta-theme here. As art historian Mitchell Merback (2012) shows in his compelling analysis of the "witnessing figures" depicted in late medieval altar-pieces of the Crucifixion scene, recognition can take on a *plurality of forms*. It is a "dawning of comprehension" and "a spectrum between seeing and blindness" that can also include "half-unfolded" disclosures, false inferencing, and "blind seeing"—all of which can stand in the way of critical discoveries. If survival is a fairly straightforward logic of dispersal and ecological opportunism, as the "zone-as-ecological wonderland" thesis suggests, then what accounts for the voids and extirpations that underpin this movement? How is extinction to be seen?

In 1859, Charles Darwin celebrated evolution's "endless forms," notably the "higher animal," as the "most exalted" object emerging from nature's war, famine, and death. In what Darwin called the

"entangled bank" of ecological interconnections and die-offs, he found the origin of species. The proximate cause of life was (some animal's) death. The proximate cause of death was (some animal's) life. The Zone's ecology prompts questions not unrelated to these seamless activities in which survival and extinction comprise two sides of the same coin. While ideas of survival and reproduction as relatively mechanistic processes of natural selection still win the day, the observable parameters of extinction—beyond a failure to adapt—have yet to be empirically worked out (Geertz 2005). Do evolution's endless formations have a time-stamp or a limit? What difference do mutagens like radiation introduce? What, we might ask, are the origins of *extinction*?

We can take the debate over the ecological integrity of the Zone as being directly relevant to how the fate of species is being inferred scientifically under various scenarios of environmental threat. The fate of the missing Chernobyl barn swallows provides a small window into the scientific challenges facing researchers in their increasingly concerted and urgent efforts to discern the causes and dynamics of species extinctions for the purposes of improving conservation strategies, particularly as they relate to climate change (Cahill et al 2012; Griffen and Drake 2009; Pimm 2009; Sæther et al. 2000, for example).

What, ecologists ask, are the appropriate scaling rules and measures for the "final decline to extinction" (Griffen and Drake 2009)? As the effects of climate change accelerate, scientists face the limitations of available tools to infer and predict when, where, and how extinction happens. Can population-based extinction processes still be knowable through statistical probabilities? Is extinction reducible to a moment when some threatened species reaches a critical limit of physiological tolerance (to heat, for example)? What does extinction, near-extinction, or the hour of extinction look like?

Mousseau and Møller can only offer conjecture as to how the decline of barn swallows in the Zone occurred (2011:43). It is possible, they write, that exposure to radiation overtaxes the bird's stores of antioxidants, needed to fight oxidative stress. Long-distance and particularly brightly colored migrants (their yellow and red feathers, crucial for attracting mates, are powered by carotenoids) ar-

---

rive already severely antioxidant-depleted at their annual breeding sites and may not have in them the extra antioxidants needed to fight radiation. They may never arrive or arrive exhausted and unable to breed in a Zone that is neither a wonderland nor wasteland, but a biogeographical place in which any number of causes and so-called stochastic factors can interact to cause a species to defy local ecological expectations.

Population viability estimates have traditionally relied on statistical analyses to determine probabilities of long-term population declines (Sæther et al. 2000:624). A variety of stochastic (or idiosyncratic) dynamics, however, confound efforts to make inferences about the *actual* time to extinction" (my italics, ibid.). Extinctions, particularly near-extinctions, are not transparent phenomena. What may look like an adaptation to increasing temperatures due to global warming—say, an animal reaches a physiological limit of heat tolerance and moves up a mountain or poleward—may be the scene of a fatal "temporal mismatch" in host-predator interactions, as hosts and predators may not migrate at a similar pace (Pimm 2009:R600; Cahill et al. 2012:2). Indeed, the mutagenic properties of climate change—if they can be characterized as such—are difficult to discern as they can produce images of both species abundance and species decline.

Mismatched timing and other idiosyncrasies of species survival make for a peculiar and non-parametric "borrowed time" scenario (Hughes et al. 2012). Modeling when and where an animal population dies off, when and under what conditions it breaks the entangled bank, so to speak, becomes a formidable task. And while there is no clear signal for extinction, there is the "disturbing possibility that there may be many extinctions due to other proximate causes long before physiological tolerances to high temperatures become predominant" (Cahill et al 2012:7). Somehow, our knowledge of extinction may never be enough.

Is the Zone an ecological wonderland or a post-industrial wasteland? Scientists and the rest of us will have to wrestle with the false dichotomies that the Zone has enlisted. Similarly, we must cut through the "blind seeing" that defines our current state of recognition of species extinction. Sudden and difficult-to-reverse processes may involve complex spatial and temporal dynamics that, we might say, have been poorly horizoned thus far. Already causing significant human and ecological disruption, the doubling of CO_2 emissions in the next few decades begs for better ways of apprehending the poorly understood dynamics of species extinction. In this space of imperfect knowledge and inexorable threat, the origins of extinction usher in a new kind of intellectual labor, a "horizoning work" (Petryna 2012), involving the construction of empirical tools and appropriate "scaling rules" (Griffen and Drake 2009) for recognizing and "maintaining a safe distance from dangerous thresholds" (Rockström et al. 2009 cited in Hughes et al. 2012:6). Horizons here act as contemporary "equipment" (Rabinow 2003) for cultivating distance as well as signaling available time for modeling, managing, and facing a complex future that is seemingly right at hand.

The centrality of such horizoning work cannot be underestimated in ecological research, as the uncertainty of previous models and unprecedented threats have prompted a search to identify "proximate factors causing extinction from climate change" (Cahill et al. 2012:2). Owing to some alluring, and maybe deadly, cognitive dissonance, the Zone is popular among disaster tourists. Yet the preoccupation with dangerous thresholds, extinction barriers, and declines also tells of the level to which horizons and horizoning work become ever-more central to our own political thought and practice. ■

ADRIANA PETRYNA *is Edmund J. and Louise W. Kahn Term Professor in Anthropology at the University of Pennsylvania. Her works include* Life Exposed: Biological Citizens after Chernobyl *and* When Experiments Travel: Clinical Trials and the Global Search for Human Subjects. *She is coeditor of* Global Pharmaceuticals: Ethics, Markets, Practices *and* When People Come First: Critical Studies in Global Health.

REFERENCES

Baker, Robert J., and Jeffrey K. Wickliffe. 2011. "Wildlife and Chernobyl: The Scientific Evidence for Minimal Impacts." *Bulletin of the Atomic Scientists,* April 14.

Cahill, Abigail E. and Matthew E. Aiello-Lammens, M. Caitlin Fisher Reid, et al. 2012. "How does Climate Change Cause Extinction?" *Proceedings of the Royal Society.* 280(1750):1-9.

Geertz, Clifford. 2005. "Very Bad News." *New York Review of Books,* March 24.

Griffen, Blaine D. and John M. Drake. 2009. "Scaling Rules for the Final Decline to Extinction." *Proceedings of the Royal Society* 276(1660):1361-1367.

Hughes, Terry P. and Cristina Linares, Vasilis Dakos, Ingrid A. van de Leemput, and Egbert H. van Nes. 2012. "Living Dangerously on Borrowed Time During Slow, Unrecognized Regime Shifts." *Trends in Ecology and Evolution,* 28(3):149-155.

Merback, Mitchell. 2012. "Recognition: Theme and Meta-Theme in Northern Renaissance Art." Lecture, School of Historical Studies, Institute for Advanced Study, Princeton, NJ. Oct 23rd.

Mousseau, Timothy A., and Anders P. Møller. 2011. "Landscape Portrait: A Look at the Impacts of Radioactive Contaminants on Chernobyl's Wildlife." *Bulletin of the Atomic Scientists* 67(2):38-46.

Petryna, Adriana. 2012. "What is a Horizon?" American Anthropological Association Meetings, San Francisco, CA, Nov 14.

Pimm, Stuart L. 2009. "Climate Disruption and Biodiversity." *Current Biology* 19(14):R595-R601.

Rabinow, Paul. 2003. *Anthropos Today: Reflections on Modern Equipment.* Princeton: Princeton University Press.

Rockstrom, Johan, et al. 2009. "Planetary Boundaries: Exploring the Safe Operating Space for Humanity." *Ecology and Society* 14(2):32.

Sæther, Bernt-Erik, Steinar Engen, Russell Lande, Peter Arcese and James N.M. Smith. 2000. "Estimating the Time to Extinction in an Island Population of Song Sparrows." *Proceedings of the Royal Society* 267(1443):621-626.

PHOTOS BY JON SULLIVAN, PDPHOTO.ORG

Amidst the debate over various culprits for honeybee colony collapse (pesticides, pathogens, parasites, habitat loss, etc.) **Chloe Silverman** asks a different question: what exactly is a healthy living system in an age of increasing vulnerability?

HOW DO YOU SPOT A HEALTHY HONEY BEE ?

In 2006, David Hackenberg, a commercial beekeeper in Pennsylvania, noticed what appeared to be a new disease in his honey bee hives. Bees are susceptible to a range of pests and pathogens with identifiable signatures, such as the parasitic *Varroa* mites that have devastated US bee colonies since the late 1980s or American foulbrood, a bacterial disease that transforms developing bee larvae nestled in their hexagonal cells into a brown mush. This was different: When Hackenberg opened up his hives, he found his colonies devastated, but without any visible evidence of sick or dying bees or brood. The adult bees had simply deserted the hives, leaving behind what appeared to be a healthy queen bee, her brood, and a handful of young bees. Hackenberg had witnessed an early instance of what would later emerge as a widespread phenomenon of overwintering colony loss in American honey bees, later dubbed Colony Collapse Disorder (CCD). Unexplained colony losses at rates of up to 36 percent have been reported each year since, although the mild winter of 2011–2012 may have contributed to lower losses than in previous years (USDA 2012).

THOSE FAMILIAR WITH THE HISTORY of disease research—in either animals or in humans—will know that convincing and widely-accepted explanations for an illness are often disproven by subsequent studies. Researchers' expectations can sometimes lead them to embrace explanations prior to definitive proof. Such readers will not be surprised that in nearly each year since 2006 a newly published research study appeared to resolve the question of CCD. In 2007, researchers associated CCD with Israeli Acute Paralysis Virus, possibly transmitted by imported packaged bees from Australia (Cox-Foster et al 2007). Researchers implicated the microsporidian *Nosema ceranae* in 2008 (Higes et al 2008), and a 2009 study proposed that nutritional stress resulting from habitat loss was the culprit (Naug 2009). In 2012 it looked like CCD was instead caused by neonicotinoids, a new class of systemic pesticides used in agriculture, which bees ingest through pollen (Henry et al 2012; Lu et al 2012). Or maybe a new parasite, phorid flies, was causing the hive abandonment seen in CCD (Core et al 2012). Each theory has had its critics, and none has been completely reliable in predicting the collapse of colonies that appear healthy beforehand. However, beekeepers want theories to have predictive power if they are going to invest the time and effort to control any particular pathogen or parasite. Miticides used to treat *Varroa* infestations, for example, carry their own costs and risks to colonies, so beekeepers have good reasons to use them sparingly if mites alone are not the cause of colony loss.

Understanding and treating the problem of colony loss might appear to be a fairly straightforward matter of identifying the cause of these distinctive symptoms: a problem that, for example, epidemiologists confront on a regular basis in both humans and animals. Samples of beeswax, larvae, and the few bees that remain in hives affected by CCD can be tested for a range of bacteria, fungi, viruses, and environmental toxins. In this view, eventually one variable will prove to be consistently present in diseased colonies and absent in healthy colonies. That single cause can then be eliminated with a tailor-made treatment. Following this logic, the US Department of Agriculture is currently funding surveys focused on identifying a cause of CCD, and Beeologics, a company purchased in 2011 by the biotech giant Monsanto, is marketing novel treatments aimed at neutralizing viruses associated with CCD.

A summary of current research on CCD could easily become a story about the different interests that promote, or dismiss, a range of possible causes of CCD. A narrative of that type would have much to say about the politics of agriculture and bee management practices. Kleinman and Suryanarayanan (2012, 18) have shown how academic priorities and industry interests can lead to a "normatively induced ignorance" in insect toxicology because certain observations and measurements related to pesticide effects are valued over others. But I want to focus on a different problem. This is the difficulty of knowing what a healthy bee colony actually looks like, or establishing the baseline against which a diseased colony might be compared.

The difficulty of precisely characterizing a healthy colony can be perplexing for beekeepers and entomologists who work closely with bees. An experienced beekeeper simply knows when a colony is healthy or sick. (In my research, I am interested in the degree to which these intuitions can be mapped onto measurable factors that entomologists might use in research). Hives with healthy bees smell "like beeswax in the sun" according to one graduate student in entomology. Sick colonies smell different, like rotting dead bees that haven't been removed from the hive according to usual bee routine because all of the other bees are occupied

> "Many of those involved with bees understand the deeply interdependent nature of bee cultivation and human culture, although they might use different terms than the ones employed by social scientists."

with being sick as well. Healthy colonies also have a recognizable sound, a contented hum very unlike the disgruntled buzz of a colony that is missing a queen (or isn't "queenright" in beekeeping parlance) because she has died from disease or injury or has been killed by workers who perceived that she was unwell.

DESPITE BEEKEEPERS' WEALTH of tacit knowledge related to colony health, it is nonetheless turning out to be hard to say what, exactly, a healthy bee colony is. One problem is that bees are social insects. Kleinman and Suryanarayanan (2012, 10 and 13) have explained how beekeepers' own assessments of colony health take into account that a bee colony is a "superorganism" not reducible to the sum of its individual members. If you open up a hive and find a bee with deformed wing virus, that is worrisome, but it doesn't necessarily mean that the entire colony is affected and will soon succumb to the disease. Honey bees are obsessed with cleanliness—they have reliable hygienic behaviors—and they are good at getting rid of sick bees. These traits are dependable enough that they produce a "social

immunity" that may even compensate for honey bees' relative absence of immune genes (Evans et al 2006). Infections have to reach a certain density in the colony to present a problem for the community as a whole. A sick colony, then, is something other than a colony with some sick bees.

But that isn't all. Entomologists have conducted surveys of hives in an attempt to catalog all of the microbes present in collapsed hives and identify pathogens present in all cases of CCD. Most colonies carry a significant burden of disease-causing organisms at any given time, with different ones dominating the mix at different times of year (Runckel et al 2011). And in many cases, these are perfectly healthy colonies, which don't appear compromised in the least. "Being sick" for a colony doesn't simply mean carrying the organisms that cause sicknesses.

Finally, there is the likelihood that the phenomenon that we call colony collapse disorder may not be caused by a single pathogen, or even a pathogen exclusively, but rather result from multiple stressors acting in concert (Neumann et al 2010). For example, ingesting systemic pesticides may lower the threshold at which bees are able to survive an attack of the intestinal microsporidium *Nosema ceranae*, making a potentially tolerable infection lethal. That sublethal doses of pesticides can be fatal when combined with other factors is a possibility left out of conventional toxicity assays (Kleinman and Suryanarayanan 2012). Development and climate change lead to meager foraging options, and researchers agree that malnourished bees succumb more rapidly to parasitic mites. *Varroa* mites, meanwhile, can act as vectors for viruses, rapidly spreading otherwise isolated infections among the bees in a hive (USDA 2005). Overwintering colony losses may be caused by different combinations of factors in different regions of the US, tracking regional differences in microorganisms, climate, pesticide use, and apicultural practice. While the problem of colony loss first identified in 2006 has persisted, cases with the classic symptoms of CCD are rare, suggesting again that colony loss may extend beyond the problem of a single, new syndrome.

At least two of these confounding factors—that harboring pathogens does not automatically mean that an individual bee or colony is sick, and that no single factor may be sufficient to cause colony collapse—have suggestive parallels in human disease ecology. Recent surveys of gut microorganisms in humans have demonstrated that healthy humans routinely carry significant numbers of disease-causing organisms, apparently kept in check by the other microflora present in a well-balanced digestive tract. Doctors have long understood that humans are more susceptible to diseases like tuberculosis when they are also malnourished. Finally, scientists are increasingly concluding that disorders like autism may never resolve into a single discrete disease entity but may represent a range of different disorders, all of which manifest in superficially similar cognitive and behavioral characteristics.

Jake Kosek (2010) reminds those concerned about the health of honey bee populations that to even discuss bee health one must remember that the honey bee is a species biologically shaped and managed by humans, who have bred bees to promote docile temperaments and high honey production, and encouraged them to live in manufactured hives—yet another wrinkle in ascertaining what a healthy bee looks like in "the wild." Bees themselves are not just bees, but configurations of human agricultural exigencies, crop management practices, beekeeper preferences, and biological constraints.

Kosek's point is significant, but it is perhaps equally important to recall that CCD occurs in the context of health crises—or at least population declines—in a range of pollinator species. These afflictions range from the rapid population declines that have devastated several US species of bumblebees to white nose disease in bats. Many of these other pollinators also experience the effects of human behavior but have not been reshaped by human artifice the way that honey bees have. It is also key that public and professional uncertainties over the cause of CCD suggest that many of those involved with bees understand the deeply interdependent nature of bee cultivation and human culture, although they might use different terms than the ones employed by social scientists.

COMPLEX AND UNEXPLAINED sicknesses reveal the tenuous nature of "healthy" states in both animals and humans. That some succumb may be an accident of location, life experience, or genetic variation. But the more central issue, and the source of some of the current uncertainty over how to characterize and address pollinator health problems, is how putatively healthy systems, be they hives or human bodies, have become increasingly vulnerable to stress, disease, and disturbance. What counts as healthy, meaning what is measurably healthy, may not be as robust as we might hope. ■

CHLOE SILVERMAN *teaches in the English Department at Penn State University.*

ACKNOWLEDGEMENTS
This material is based upon work supported by the National Science Foundation under Grant No. 1058933. Any opinions, findings, and conclusions or recommendations expressed in this material are those of the author and do not necessarily reflect the views of the National Science Foundation. I am grateful to Christina Grozinger, Elina Lastro Niño, Nancy Ostiguy, and Bob Vitalis for their corrections and input on drafts of this essay. Any errors are, of course, my own.

REFERENCES
USDA Research Service. 2005. "Viruses." Accessed September 14, 2012 at: http://www.ars.usda.gov/Services/docs.htm?docid=7461&pf=1&cg_id=0

Core, Andrew, Charles Runckel, Jonathan Ivers, Christopher Quock, et al. 2012. "A New Threat to Honey Bees, the Parasitic Phorid Fly, *Apocephalus borealis*." *PloS one* 7(1): e29639.

Cox-Foster, Diana L., Sean Conlan, Edward C. Holmes, Gustavo Palacios, et al. 2007. "A Metagenomic Survey of Microbes in Honey Bee Colony Collapse Disorder." *Science*, 318(283):283–287.

Evans, Jay Daniel, Katherine Aronstein, Yanping Chen, Charles Hetru, et al., 2006. "Immune Pathways and Defense Mechanisms in Honey Bees, *Apis mellifera. Insect Molecular Biology*, 15(5):645–656.

Higes, Mariano, Raquel Martín-Hernández, Cristina Botías, Encarna Garrido Bailón, et al. 2008. "How Natural Infection by *Nosema ceranae* Causes Honeybee Colony Collapse." *Environmental Microbiology*. 10(10):2659–2669.

Kleinman, Daniel Lee and Sainath Suryanarayanan. 2012. "Dying Bees and the Social Production of Ignorance." *Science, Technology, and Human Values*. May 3rd. DOI: 10.1177/0162243912442575.

Kosek, Jake. 2010. "Ecologies of Empire: On the New Uses of the Honeybee." *Cultural Anthropology*, 25(4):650–678.

Lu, Chensheng, Kenneth M. Warchol, and Richard A. Callahan. 2012. "*In Situ* Replication of Honeybee Colony Collapse Disorder." *Bulletin of Insectology*, 65(1):n.p.

Naug, Dhruba. 2009. "Nutritional Stress Due to Habitat Loss May Explain Recent Honeybee Colony Collapses." *Biological Conservation*, 142(10):2369–2372.

Neumann, Peter and Norman L. Carreck. 2010. "Guest Editorial: Honey Bee Colony Losses." *Journal of Apicultural Research*, 49(1):1–6.

Runckel, Charles, Michelle L. Flenniken, Juan C. Engel, J. Graham Ruby, et al. 2011. "Temporal Analysis of the Honey Bee Microbiome Reveals Four Novel Viruses and Seasonal Prevalence of Known Viruses, *Nosema*, and *Crithidia*." *PLoS One*, 6(6):e20656.

UN**BEAR**ABLE FUTURE

PHOTO: KARYN RODE/USFWS, 2009

One of the more spectacular signs of the onset of climate change is the decline of the polar bear population. But is it really in decline? **Etienne Benson** traces the long and controversial history of modeling the future population of polar bears.

"TWO RESEARCH SCIENTISTS KILL FIVE BEARS" was the headline splashed across the front page of the *Tundra Times* on April 8, 1966. The perpetrators were Vagn Flyger and Martin Schein, biologists from Maryland who had just spent three weeks on Alaska's North Slope trying to tranquilize and tag polar bears. According to Flyger and Schein's own later report, they had in fact accidentally killed only four bears (Flyger 1967: 53). Of the thirty-eight they had pursued by aircraft over the sea ice near Barrow, Alaska, they had managed to hit seven with darts laden with a powerful muscle relaxant, of which four died of overdoses and two were unaffected. The only specimen of *Ursus maritimus* they managed to successfully tranquilize, tag and release was killed soon after by an Inuit hunter who complained that the dye the scientists had used had spoiled the skin.

The study was meant to be the first phase in a long-term project exploring the species' population ecology, but the bears' death brought the plan to an abrupt end. Arctic science, Flyger and Schein had discovered, was a difficult and dangerous game. Seeking to build a scientific sensor that could detect threats to the species' survival, they had proven only that research itself could be a threat.

Flyger and Schein had first proposed capturing and tagging polar bears a year earlier, when biologists from the United States, Canada, Denmark, Norway, and the Soviet Union met in Fairbanks for the first international scientific meeting on the polar bear. The meeting was motivated by alarming claims that fewer than 8,000 bears remained worldwide and by concern about the rise of airplane-based trophy hunting in Alaska. The ultimate goal of the meeting, as Alaskan Senator E.L. Bartlett reminded the assembled scientists, was to produce a "machinery to gather, evaluate, and distribute information for the future" (Bartlett 1966: 3-4). Its immediate result,

however, was to solidify the consensus that existing estimates of polar bear populations were, as the delegation from Alaska put it, "based on tenuous assumptions and extrapolation of fragmentary data" (Delegation of the United States, 1966: 45). Global estimates ranged from a low of 5,000 to a high of more than 20,000 bears.

Although Flyger and Schein moved on, other biologists subsequently improved on their efforts as part of a campaign to collect data and develop population models that would ensure the polar bear's survival in the face of a rapidly industrializing Arctic. Coordinating their work through the Polar Bear Specialist Group of the International Union for the Conservation of Nature, they eventually met with a large measure of success in both the political and scientific realms (Fikkan et al. 2010).

The outrage sparked by Flyger and Schein's research was only one of many controversies that have flared up around research on polar bears since the initial push for a new "machinery" of surveillance and prediction in the 1960s. Some of these controversies have centered on the methods scientists use to gather data on polar bear numbers and movements, particularly the use of tranquilizers, tags, and other invasive techniques criticized by many animal rights activists, wilderness activists, and indigenous hunters, albeit for different reasons. Other controversies have centered on the models and simulations biologists have developed to estimate past, present, and future polar bear populations. Conservationists and hunters have often disputed these as producing population estimates that are either too high or too low. Such disputes are in essence fights about the future—not just over different visions of the future, but over the very methods that are used to envision what the future might and should look like.

The polar bear's imagined future has gone through several phases since the alarm was first sounded in the

1960s. By the 1980s, on the basis of tagging data collected by Flyger and Schein's more successful colleagues, most biologists and conservationists had concluded that the species was under no immediate threat of extinction. The models they used to interpret those data provided the basis for management decisions, including the setting of annual hunting quotas that would not threaten the survival of particular subpopulations. According to these models, certain populations in Canada, which was home to the vast majority of the world's polar bears, were robust enough to sustain not just indigenous hunting but also a commercial trophy hunt.

In 1994, the U.S. Congress, responding to pressure from sport-hunters and Canadian provincial governments and to assurances from scientists that Canada's bears were being sustainably managed, re-opened American borders to the import of polar bear trophies. This amendment of the 1972 Marine Mammal Protection Act allowed hunters to import nearly 1,000 trophies from Canada in the decade after 1997, when the first permits were issued.[1] The decision was opposed by many environmentalists and animal rights activists, but the machinery of monitoring that polar bear biologists had been building since the 1960s seemed to be functioning smoothly.

At the very moment when the problem of determining how many polar bears could be harvested each year without threatening the species' survival seemed to have been solved, however, biologists began to worry about another, quite different threat. In 2007, responding to a petition and lawsuit from the Center for Biological Diversity, the U.S. Fish and Wildlife Service commissioned a series of reports by climate scientists and a leading American polar bear biologist to determine whether the warming of the Arctic climate might threaten the species' long-term survival. Collectively the reports represented a path-breaking attempt to merge the techniques of population modeling that wildlife biologists had been developing for decades with climate scientists' global circulation models. The reports concluded that there was a high probability of drastic declines in the global polar bear population by mid-century because of shrinking Arctic summer sea ice (Amstrup et al., 2007). This conclusion served as the basis for the Fish and Wildlife Service's decision in 2008 to designate the polar bear as "threatened" under the Endangered Species Act—that is, not immediately at risk of extinction, but likely to become so in the "foreseeable future."

The language of the ESA has, not surprisingly, opened the door for critics to challenge the Fish and Wildlife Service's definition of "foreseeable." The "threatened" listing decision was and has remained the target of attacks by climate skeptics, trophy hunters, and some of Canada's First Nations communities, who lost a significant source of revenue when the listing put an end to the trophy import program begun in the mid-1990s and who often could see no evidence themselves of polar bear population declines (Freeman and Wenzel, 2006). Some of these opponents have argued that the science of climate change that contributed to the listing decision is fundamentally different from the wildlife biology with which they are familiar—more speculative, more dependent on ungrounded assumptions, more likely to spark what they see as alarmist overreactions, more oriented to the undecided future than to the observable present.

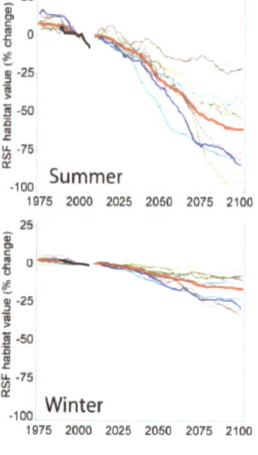

Like Sarah Palin, the one-time governor of Alaska and vice-presidential candidate, these critics argue that the designation of the species as threatened with extinction is unjustified because it is based "on uncertain modeling of possible effects" (Palin, 2008). Climate change may be happening and conservation is in any case essential, they argue, but decisions about how to prevent it or adapt to it are best left in the hands of local people and scientists wielding well-established research methods. This is a battle as much over who has the right and ability to predict the "foreseeable future" as it is over which future should be pursued.

Because of climate change, the polar bear has once again become the focus of international attention and a symbol for the possible futures of nonhuman life on a human-dominated Earth. However charismatic the polar bear may be, it is easy to wonder whether all of this attention is justified. Many conservation biologists have criticized the popular focus on certain high-profile species to the neglect of broader ecosystems, even as they have cannily deployed pandas, polar bears, and other large, exotic creatures to raise funds and advance their cause (Lorimer, 2007). The uniqueness of the polar bear's case in epistemological terms might also be doubted. Seen through the lens of the climate wars, the question of polar bear extinction might seem like a minor skirmish that simply replicates, in miniature, grander battles over climate change models, economic impacts, and the fate of the entire planet (Edwards, 2010). All that was particular about the polar bear's uncertain future might seem now to have been subsumed by the one great challenge of establishing consensus and motivating action to prevent climate catastrophe.

If it is possible to see polar bear conservation as a special case of the response to climate change, however, it is also possible to see climate change as simply another episode in a half-century history of attempting to predict, using the best scientific methods available, the polar bear's future. In the context of this history, there is much about the new debates that seems awfully similar to the old ones. Now as before, scientific data and models are seen as necessary for making conservation decisions, although they are rarely if ever determinative. The undisputed importance of the models makes them targets of close scrutiny, and the more they are scrutinized, the clearer their limitations become. For polar bear biologists, disputes over "tenuous assumptions and extrapolation of fragmentary data" amidst urgent calls to action predate

---

1   A list of all applications for polar bear trophy import permits can be found at
http://polarbearfeed.etiennebenson.com/visualizations

"These models remain highly disputable—dim and flickering lights in the face of an obscure future."

by decades Al Gore's *An Inconvenient Truth* and the listing of the polar bear as "threatened."

The occasional irruption of a scandal over research methods is also nothing new. Determining safe and effective doses of tranquilizing drugs may have been replaced by fine-tuning the parameters of climate models, but narratives about the risks of modernity, the limits of certainty, the hope of staving off unwelcome change, and the necessity of embracing new technologies and scientific methods remain largely unchanged. Moreover, recent calls for taking responsibility for the Earth in the era of the Anthropocene (e.g., Marris, 2011) echo the understanding of "management" advanced by biologists at the Fairbanks meeting fifty years ago. Above all, uncertainty about the future and the eternally deferred hope of a final scientific resolution to that uncertainty remain constitutive aspects of modernity and of the project of conservation, which has always been about preserving valued aspects of the past against the inevitable onslaught of the future. Despite efforts by scientists to shore up their predictions with more data and more robust models, such predictions remain highly disputable—dim and flickering lights in the face of an obscure future. There is no reason not to believe that climate change poses real threats of a novel nature, but there is nothing especially new about the uncertainty it brings, or about the fear that what that uncertainty hides is an unbearable (and potentially bearless) future.

Looking back at Flyger and Schein's ill-fated efforts on the Arctic ice in 1966 and the context in which they took place helps to put today's disputes over polar bears and polar bear science in perspective. Scientists are still trying to produce what Bartlett called a "machinery ... for the future" that will make it possible to preserve some of the most valued aspects of the present, including the existence of polar bears. They are still occasionally making mistakes, even if those mistakes are less likely to involve the lethal overdosing of four or five bears than they were in the mid-1960s. Those whose lives may be affected by that machinery are still asking questions about how much it will cost to build, about who has the ability and the right to wield it, and how the information it produces will be put to use. ∎

ETIENNE BENSON *is a Research Scholar at the Max Planck Institute for the History of Science in Berlin. He is the author of* Wired Wilderness: Technologies of Tracking and the Making of Modern Wildlife *(Johns Hopkins University Press, 2010).*

REFERENCES

Amstrup, Steven C., Marcot, Bruce G. and David C. Douglas. 2007. *Forecasting the Range-wide Status of Polar Bears at Selected Times in the 21st Century.* Administrative Report, U.S. Geological Survey, available online at http://www.usgs.gov/newsroom/special/polar_bears/

Arctic Institute of North America. 1966. "A Proposal for Research on the Ecology of the Polar Bear," in *Proceedings of the First International Scientific Meeting on the Polar Bear*, Fairbanks, Alaska, 6-10 September 1965. Washington, D.C.: U.S. Department of the Interior, p. 59.

Bartlett, Edward Lewis. 1966. "Opening Address," in *Proceedings of the First International Scientific Meeting on the Polar Bear*, Fairbanks, Alaska, 6-10 September 1965. Washington, D.C.: U.S. Department of the Interior, pp. 3-4.

Bernstein, Adam. 2006. "Vagn Flyger, 83; Biologist Was Expert on Squirrels," *Washington Post*, January 12.

Delegation of the United States. 1966. "The Polar Bear in Alaska," in *Proceedings of the First International Scientific Meeting on the Polar Bear*, Fairbanks, Alaska, 6-10 September 1965 Washington, D.C.: U.S. Department of the Interior, pp. 43-54.

Edwards, Paul. 2010. *A Vast Machine: Computer Models, Climate Data, and the Politics of Global Warming.* Cambridge, MA: MIT Press.

Fikkan, Anne, Osherenko, Gail and Alexander Arikainen. 1993. "Polar Bears: The Importance of Simplicity," in Oran R. Young and Gail Osherenko, eds., *Polar Politics: Creating International Environmental Regimes.* Ithaca: Cornell University Press, pp. 96-151.

Flyger, Vagn. 1967. "Polar Bear Studies During 1966," *Arctic* 20(1):53.

Francis, H. to A.P. Crary, 1967. Box 6, Entry 33, April 7, Office of Antarctic Programs, Records of the Program Director for Biology and Medicine. National Science Foundation, Record Group 307, National Archives and Records Administration, College Park, MD.

Freeman, M. M. R. and G. W. Wenzel. 2006. "The Nature and Significance of Polar Bear Conservation Hunting in the Canadian Arctic," *Arctic* 59(1):21-30.

Godbout, Oscar. 1966. "Scientists to Study Polar Bears Via Transmitters in Orbiting Satellite," *New York Times*, June 29.

Lorimer, Jamie. 2005. "Nonhuman Charisma," *Environment and Planning D: Society and Space* 25(5):911-932.

Marris, Emma. 2011. *Rambunctious Garden: Saving Nature in a Post-Wild World.* New York: Bloomsbury.

Palin, Sarah. 2008. "Bearing Up," *New York Times*, 5 January.

HETEROGENEOUS NARRATIONS OF AN ONGOING DISASTER

How did plastic garbage patches floating in the ocean become an object of public concern? BAPTISTE MONSAINGEON relates the media campaigns that turned the gradual accumulation of oceanic waste from an abstract and imperceptible concern to a dire emergency requiring immediate attention.

OCEANS *of* PLASTIC

Have you ever heard of the "garbage patches" that float in the middle of the oceans? Yes, presumably. Marine litter is today is considered one key element of human impact on ecosystems at a global scale (Law et al., 2010). In 2011, an emblematic mark of that recognition came from the United Nation Environmental Program (UNEP) that featured marine plastic debris as one of its major issues of the year (Kershaw et al., 2011).[1] But this issue has not always been a prominent object of international concern.

In 1972, Carpenter and Smith were the first scientists to describe unexpected plastic debris concentration in western Atlantic.[2] However, for more than two decades, this news rarely entered mainstream media. It was only forty years after these first scientific investigations that plastic marine pollution 'officially' became a global issue. If the phenomenon has been known for so long, how is it that it only recently became a matter of public concern? What specific set of events allowed plastic debris in oceans to be considered as an "ongoing catastrophe"? How can the emergence of this public awareness be understood?

Neither strictly natural, nor strictly social, plastic accumulations in oceans can be described as a type of "hybrid" (Latour, 1993). Above all, these floating phenomena are a product of time: On the one hand, they became a threat for ecosystems over decades of intensive consumption and disposal of plastic items; on the other hand, more than forty years have been necessary to build them as "matter of concern" (Latour, 2004). The complex process of producing this public issue is the concern of this article.

THE "PLASTIC THREAT" IN OCEANS

Generally, if anthropogenic debris appears as an offence to "nature", it is first in pure aesthetic, phenomenological terms: Here, perception of abjection expresses above all a conflict between an idealized view of "natural" landscape and a kind of culturally produced desire to protect its apparent status as untouched wilderness. Beyond the unpleasant experience of encountering 'polluted' waters—whether in the form of treading on soiled beaches, wandering past wrecked cars in rivers, or spotting floating bottles in the ocean surf, we could all potentially agree that the silent and invisible accumulation of these items over time would

---

1   UNEP 2011 year book accessible online : http://www.
     unep.org/yearbook/2011/pdfs/plastic_debris_in_the_
     ocean.pdf

2   E. J. Carpenter, K. L. Smith, Plastics on the Sargasso Sea
     surface. *Science* 175, 1240-1241 (1972). Their work was
     focused on Atlantic Ocean, and specifically on Sargasso
     Sea. But, in 1973, an other research team described
     same phenomenon in Pacific: Venrick, E. L and al.
     (1973): Man-made objects on the surface of the central
     North Pacific Ocean. *Nature,* 241, 271

contribute to a global threat. But with quasi-imperceptible phenomenon such as garbage patches, some differences have to be examined. The process of accumulation in the oceans could be ignored as long as most of the debris floated far from human life centers. Because of the striking contrast between those tiny little pieces and the immensity of the oceans, the accumulation of plastic debris has been a slow and silent process of gradual invasion covering a large surface area of the oceans. Therefore time is a key actor.

Despite an initial lack of consistent data, scientists now agree on a range of understandings of the harms related to presence of plastics in the marine environment, from this garbage's impacts on wildlife to its effects on human health (Thompson et al., 2009). Indeed, one key threat now understood related to this pollution in oceans is the slow fragmentation of plastic objects, driven by currents in multiple giant vortexes around the globe. As a result of

MIDWAY—MESSAGE FROM THE GYRE. On Midway Atoll, a remote cluster of islands more than 2000 miles from the nearest continent, the detritus of our mass consumption surfaces in an astonishing place: inside the stomachs of thousands of dead baby albatrosses. The nesting chicks are fed lethal quantities of plastic by their parents, who mistake the floating trash for food as they forage over the vast polluted Pacific Ocean.

PHOTO AND CAPTION TEXT CHRIS JORDAN

this dispersion, satellites are unable to capture immediately legible images of these concentrations. Micro-debris can only be measured in "at-sea observation", consisting, in broad outline, in "raking over" oceans' surface with plankton nets. Despite scientists' painstaking efforts over 20 years to collect these observations, this type of factual evidence was not successful in raising public awareness of the marine litter issue.

Standing on the edge of human perception, far from everyday public concerns, the quasi-abstracted nature of gradual accumulation is one of the reasons why campaigns in the media were needed to transform plastic accumulation into a prioritized global environmental issue. In the 2000s, a number of poignant pictures spread by mainstream press and websites played a key role in mobilizing of public opinion. From the Albatros' stomach-full-of-plastic-caps to the turtle-deformed-by-a-plastic-ring, iconic pictures recognized by growing numbers of people around the world today connect improper disposal of plastic litter with a growing threat for wildlife. In a way, these animals acted as early "sentinels", exemplifying for large audiences an encroaching danger.

But, in our case, words, at least as much as pictures, could have played a central role in the emergence of plastic accumulation concern.

A POSTMODERN COLUMBUS

At the end of the 1990s, Captain Charles Moore, the founder of Algalita Marine Research Foundation, described to Curtis Ebbesmeyer—a famous oceanographer and specialist of ocean currents and floating objects—his encounter with staggering concentrations of plastic litter accumulated in the middle of the Eastern Pacific on a large surface area. The oceanographer nicknamed it "the great Pacific garbage patch". The narration of this strange confrontation sounded like a pale caricature of the great discovery of the new world: Moore, the Columbus of post-modern times, discovered a new "continent", a New World built by the unintentional consequences of humans' action. Media from around the world reported the "discovery", first carefully then more ardently. That Moore's claims lacked scientific evidence, including quantified data about the size of these "patches", seemed to be a sufficient reason to doubt this "story" as the biased spin of a sensationalizing activist. Yet the tangible dimension of the word "patch" helped to spread the powerful mythical image of an archipelago of "garbage islands" scattered in the middle of the ocean. In the wake of Moore's intervention,

From the Albatros' stomach-full-of-plastic-caps to the turtle-deformed-by-a-plastic-ring, iconic

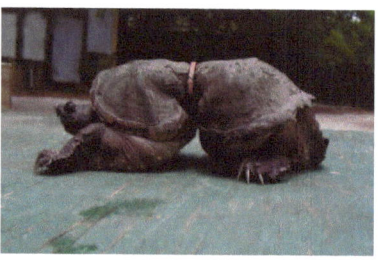

pictures recognized by growing numbers of people around the world today connect improper disposal of plastic litter with a growing threat for wildlife.

architects in the Netherlands in the early 2000s launched a project named the "recycled island", which presented the recycling of garbage patches as a kind of "promised land" for climate refugees.[3]

The "patches" metaphor travelled beyond activist circles. Oceanographers and marine biologists soon developed model simulations of the distribution of marine litter in the main oceanic gyres. Interestingly, the production and circulation of these scientific representations markedly increased after Moore's re-invention of plastic accumulation in oceans (Leichter, 2011). These scientific *bricolages* (Levi-Strauss, 1962), oscillating between the collection of empirical data and their extrapolation in theoretical models of dispersion, produce pictures that precisely materialized the dispersal of plastics on seas, and participated in the spread of a conception of plastic accumulation as solid "patches".

Over the course of ten short years, we witnessed a semantic shift in the appellation of these accumulations. In part because the word "patches" came to be criticized by scientists—and by Moore himself—as a misleading metaphor, some soon suggested an alternate name: "plastic soups". From a solid to a liquid metaphor, this new denomination was supposed to better reflect to the inconsistent, quasi-immaterial, and hardly perceptible nature of plastic accumulation. But, the "plastic soup" moniker also drew attention to a new danger absent from the earlier metaphor, namely the problem of plastic toxics components' bioaccumulation in the food chain.

Moreover, this new expression points to a movement of ongoing anthropization of a hypothetic immaculate nature. If some parts of oceans can be compared to a plastic soup, their fluctuating frontiers are interpretable as a way to foreshadow a blurring of the limits between nature and culture. In other words, this new view presents oceans as a human product in progress, a 'toxic soup'.

PERSPECTIVES

Ironically, while they became a public concern, concentrations of marine litter have been perceived as something at once threatening as desirable: The accumulation was a threat because the process immediately appeared as a potential risk for ecosystems; however, it was at the same time desirable as it posed a new challenge for scientists and publics to mobilize around.

What has to be underlined here is the equivoque position of scientific discourses around the metaphors that make it appear as a public concern: If these buzz words can on occasion mislead the ac-

---

3 Cf. http://www.recycledisland.com/

tual comprehension of a given phenomenon, they also fully participate in its emergence as a global issue. Thus, plastic marine debris has become a global concern through the weaving of perceptible and threatening evidences, lead by a kind of unwitting cooperation between eco-activists, the media, politicians and scientists. But, the hermetic ethical barriers between these poles of the debate are just apparent: With figures like Moore, who presents himself as both an activist and a scientist, the porosity between these different levels of engagement becomes visible. Indeed, activist-scientists are (politically and economically) interested in seeing their area of specialization grow into a global concern. As central components of alert devices, the formulation and dissemination of denomination processes play a crucial role.

In competing attempts to represent the multiple aspects of the marine litter problem, the tropes of "soup" and "patches" both literally and figuratively emerged as parts of a complex issue. The UNEP reports that at least 70 percent of marine litter actually sinks (Kershaw et al., 2011). Thus, any attempt to "clean" the surface of oceans would be primarily ephemeral and cosmetic. But despite the lack of comparable worldwide measures of plastic concentration, and despite the absence of scientific proof of human contamination by plastics' toxics (Thompson et al., 2009), "garbage patches" happen, and the recognition of their existence seems, day after day, to call for new solutions. As recent campaigns organized by NGOs demonstrate,[4] the metaphors have created impetus for new responses to a re-conceptualized problem: from cleaning beaches to sorting garbage, from avoiding plastics to banning them altogether. But, facing a problem that has been monitored by scientists for 40 years, are these emerging "everyday practices" adequate responses to the "disaster"?

To become "matters of concern", oceans of plastic had to be concretized through metaphors of consistency. In this way, it is as if sentinel devices needed to build a kind of thickness of matter to be able to launch alerts. In our case, that thickness stays profoundly ambivalent: Resulting from the combination of heterogeneous narrations, it seems to be a product of a kind of contemporary bricolage, closer to the myths of the "savage mind" than to the certitudes of engineers. ■

BAPTISTE MONSAINGEON *is a PhD candidate based at the Centre d'Etudes des Techniques, des Connaissances et des Pratiques at the University of Paris I, and is a member of the Watch the Waste project.*

REFERENCES:
Carpenter, Edward. J., and Smith K.L. 1972. "Plastics on the Sargasso Sea surface", *Science* 175(4027):1240–1241.
Kershaw, Peter, Saido Katsuhiko, Sangjin Lee et al. 2011. "Plastic debris in the ocean", *UNEP 2011 yearbook,* pp.20–33, available online: http://www.unep.org/yearbook/2011/pdfs/plastic_debris_in_the_ocean.pdf
Latour, Bruno. 1991. *We Have Never Been Modern.* Cambridge, MA: Harvard University Press.
Latour, Bruno. 2004. "Why has Critique run out of Steam? From Matters of Fact to Matters of Concern", *Critical Inquiry,* 30(2):225–248.
Leichter, James. J. 2011. "Investigating the Accumulation of Plastic Debris in the North Pacific Gyre", *Interdisciplinary Studies on Environmental Chemistry, 5 (Marine Environmental Modeling & Analysis)*:251–259.
Levi-Strauss, Claude. 1962. *La pensée sauvage,* Paris: Plon.
Thompson, Richard C., Charles J. Moore, Frederick S. vom Saal et al. 2009. "Plastics, the environment and human health: current consensus and future trends." *Philosophical Transactions of the Royal Society in Biological Sciences.* 364(1526):2153–2166.

---

4   Cf. for instance, Surfrider europe marine litter campaign : http://www.surfrider.eu/en/communication/ad-campaigns.html

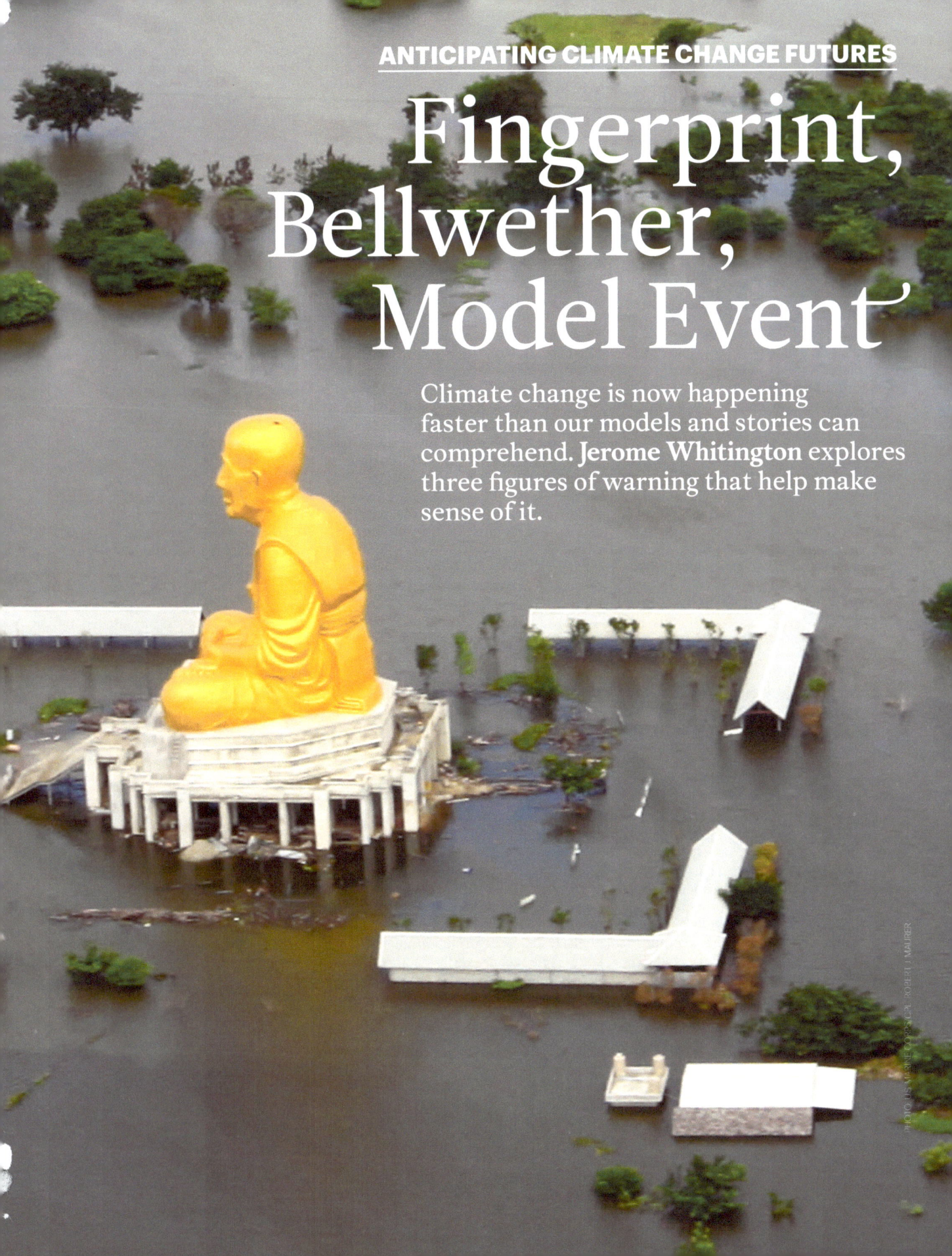

Fingerprint, Bellwether, Model Event

Climate change is now happening faster than our models and stories can comprehend. **Jerome Whitington** explores three figures of warning that help make sense of it.

Climate watchers over the past decade have witnessed momentous ecological changes accompanying the current rise in average Earth temperatures. What was before experienced as predictions about polar and glacial ice loss, ecological shifts and intensified weather is now increasingly confirmed. Moreover, the real-world changes in many cases are outpacing the modeled scenarios. These transformations afford the anthropologist climate watcher an opportunity to ask about the expert vernaculars through which expert and political actors apprehend threatening ecological futures. I explore here three terms, *the bellwether, the climate fingerprint,* and *the model event,* that enable precise thinking about the implications of climate change.

The climate fingerprint has a limited but crucial application. The fingerprint refers to a class of methodologies to assess whether real world events like droughts or changes in species ecology can be attributed to climate change. Taking climate change as a problem related to small but persistent changes, they look for distinctive data signatures that validate global circulation models while providing specificity to anticipated local changes. As Gramelsberger and Feichter (2011, pg. 9) put it, the "scientific concept of climate [is] a mathematical construct that cannot be experienced directly." Validation is critical in a context in which global circulation models are unable to capture fine-grained local dynamics, and in which a premium is placed on correlating mathematical pattern with qualitative real world transformations. Learning to trust models implies an ethics of circumspection in how they are used.

Biologists Parmesan and Yohe have provided a methodology for identifying a climate fingerprint, or signature, across large amounts of ecological data that may contain a weak climate warming signal. Their work seeks to isolate whether global warming is changing individual species' and communities' location, composition, and timing of species interactions (phenology). "Most local changes," they write, "are idiosyncratic and consist of noise when scaled up; however, atmospheric carbon dioxide levels have risen nearly uniformly across the globe" (Parmesan and Yohe 2003, pg. 39). Only the global analysis of many different species can confirm the long wave transformation. They draw on studies of 484 species

(or groups) for phenological changes and 460 species for range distribution and community composition. Eighty seven percent of the former and 81% of the latter were observed to change as predicted, providing a strong validation of the models.

Reciprocally, fingerprinting diffuses the old language of causality, for it makes little sense to say climate change has 'caused' a given weather or ecological event. One example of fingerprinting is to model 'retro-dictions' of extremely warm nights. CO_2 prevents nighttime cooling, unlike increased solar radiation, which is one preferred climate skeptic argument against the science. Comparing modeled and measured increases in extremely warm nights validates global circulation models, but it also makes clear that publics may expect too much local specificity from a science of global change (e.g. Karl et al. 2008). Whether a given event was 'caused' by climate change places undue emphasis on causality for weather systems that are always defined by a great many contingent variables. Climate science provides not detailed predictions with precise causes, but modeled scenarios that allow for deliberate work in the present, oriented toward an anticipated future.

In this context, the bellwether has been offered as an anticipatory device often used interchangeably with the term sentinel. Etymologically, the wether is a sheep and a member of a flock (OED Online 2012); the bellwether is the lead sheep which, with a bell around its neck, allows the shepherd to know the whereabouts of the flock even if it is out of visual range. The metaphor is explicitly pastoral and pattern-orientated rather than tuned to identify the specificity of a martial threat.

With respect to climate change, the bellwether grammar applies to two distinct classes of phenomena, small streams, arctic lakes, water catchments and certain species on the one hand, which are harbingers of ecological change across particularly delicate threshold ecologies; and large scale geophysical ice formations, such as the Antarctic Peninsula, glaciers or, especially, the Arctic polar ice cap. The latter are singular entities in a way the former are not, and they speak more directly to the socio-technical dimensions of nonlinear planetary events in which a small amount of warming might have dramatic consequences.

Nowhere are the emerging effects of

climate change more acute than in the Arctic, where temperatures have increased at twice the global average, and predictions of largely ice-free summers recently have been moved forward to as early as 2030 (e.g. Wang and Overland 2009). While the extent of Arctic sea ice has definitively retreated, the events have also posed questions about the density of ice and the climate feedbacks it helps maintain.

"The Arctic Ocean is now opening to the greater global society in ways that were completely unanticipated a decade ago," write the authors of 'Climate Change and International Security: The Arctic as Bellwether' (Huebert et al. 2012, pg. 6). "The ice that has long maintained the Arctic as a uniquely placid international space is receding rapidly." An ice mass with relational significance, once tacitly stabilizing geopolitics, now makes explicit new potential for military, shipping and resource expansion. Planetary geopolitical ecology has become the subject of deliberate anticipation among the eight circumpolar countries.

If one asks what the Arctic is a bellwether for, the answer provided is that "climate change is a national and international security interest in the traditional strategic sense." The heightened anxiety/opportunism announced by the climate bellwether may be symbolized by the Russian planting of a flag on the sea floor at the North Pole in 2007, or Dmitry Medvedev claiming, "Our first and main priority is to turn the Arctic into Russia's resource base for the 21st century" (Huebert et al. 2012, pg. 1, 31).

The bellwether demonstrates that climate change establishes its presence largely in terms of uncertain futures, where uncertainty is itself especially generative. In this sense, the bellwether does double-duty. Whatever the accuracy of their interpretation, circumpolar nations have no doubt that climate change is a high-stakes play advanced far beyond official United Nations discourse. Their anticipation itself, more than biophysical changes per se, is the most immediate and least predictable dimension of a militarized geopolitical ecology. If the climate is a wild card, what might be expected from these different governments?

Medvedev is speaking not only about mineral resources, but especially about the anticipation of vast undiscovered petroleum reserves still frozen out of energy markets due to the engineering challenges of underwater Arctic drilling. One bell-wether event ricocheted through business media in 2011, with Exxon signing a long-term Arctic exploration agreement with the Russian state petroleum firm Rosneft, with an indicative value of some $500 billion. That's not small change for a future supposedly oriented toward the divestment of fossil energy industries and the radical geologies they practice.

New fossil energy investment is only one of several powerful feedbacks where one can witness the opportunistic/anxious anticipation of global change. The primary atmospheric feedback is that polar ice reflects solar radiation during the endless summer days and, as the ice melts, the dark waters in its place exacerbate the heating effect. Another is the increasingly thawed permafrost, which threatens to vent additional billions of tons of methane, the powerful greenhouse gas, into the atmosphere. There is a fair amount of scary sensationalism on this point, with activist publics signaling somewhat frantically toward an unlikely runaway greenhouse effect.

Notably, the final feedback concerns the Arctic as exploratory domain for fantastic geoengineering proposals. Solar radiation management, which proposes a different sort of radical geology, would inject aerosols into the stratosphere to block sunlight and limit warming. In that case, the immediate effects of warming might be forestalled for a time but, since global CO_2 emissions continue to rise unabated, a commitment to planetary engineering seems to only preserve the momentum of financed fossil energy futures foretold in Medvedev's promise.

In the meantime, the authors note that several of the circumpolar states are investing into Arctic military capacity far beyond what is needed for normal policing activity. Such a race for resources secured by stock militarization implies a commitment to the doxa of conventional geopolitics. No party to the Arctic can safely assume the others will accept docilely a carbon-constrained future orchestrated by a United Nations convention that threatens economic growth no less than the raw terms of geopolitical claims to power. Canada and Russia, both having abandoned the Kyoto Protocol, have clearly staked their game-theoretical futures on expansive fossil energy reserves. Russia's fossil energy production is already some 20% of its economy, while Canada's commitment to oil sands makes

it an emerging circumpolar petrostate.

The Arctic as bellwether hinges on whether circumpolar geopolitical brokers expect that climate change is real and underway. Through their committed activities, their own anticipation about climate change becomes an integral part of the event. How do assumptions of climate science accelerate feedbacks of human apprehension? To what extent does climate anticipation threaten to spin itself out of control? The bellwether is an anticipatory device that treats the real world as a simulation because it treats other people's expectations as diagnosing the actuality of climate change. As with all modeling operations, it traces scenarios rather than formulating predictions. It makes urgent a present of potential actions rather than determining a future of definite outcomes. The Arctic as bellwether implies a tricky, non-obvious task

This is what the Arctic is a bellwether for: *"Climate change is a national and international security interest in the traditional strategic sense."*

of unwinding from a dangerous historical situation of committed militarization and fossil energy dependence.

The bellwether is very close to the idea of a sentinel species, but it has a different range of applications. The sentinel, a martial herald of emerging disease surveillance, helps show that a threat is a kind of risk that cannot be managed within the bounds of social forms such as insurance (Keck 2010; Collier and Lakoff 2008). Certain species do purport to tell the future of climate—most notably penguins (Boersma 2008)—but the expectation placed on the bellwether is different. The pastoral bellwether is neutral and leaves open that some Arctic actors view climate change as a welcome opportunity.

What is asked of a soothsayer can be viewed as a record of one's horizon of expectation. For the disease sentinel, what remains unknown is the given point and time at which an anticipated pathogen might appear, and its precise nature. The climate bellwether anticipates a shift in pattern, not the discrete threat of a transformed organism such as a virus. The

penguin as a sentinel species is clearly responding to environmental transformations, including trends like climate change. But does it announce that climate change has arrived? Does it communicate what is in store for the rest of us? Indeed, they are better understood as *marine* sentinels, and Boersma, the scientist who has named them as such, uses their predicament to demonstrate the multiple stresses on oceans, including climate change. I view polar bears, in contrast to penguins, as communication devices, not sentinels. Rhetorically they function to convince, not to interrogate or problematize a future. Designating a sentinel or a bellwether implies clarifying one's assumptions and learning how to ask which questions are important.

A model event is a real world environmental event, such as an extreme flood, hurricane or drought, which makes clear

the stakes of long-term weather changes in non-obvious ways. I have developed the term to understand experiences of flooding in central Thailand during Oct-Nov 2011, which demonstrated Bangkok's unique vulnerabilities even though the flood's main proximate causes were mismanagement and inadequate urban infrastructure (Whitington n.d.). The model event reveals what climate futures may look like, and forces people to assess their relation to that vulnerability in terms of the specificity of a real event.

Part of the Thai event stemmed from a widespread insurance failure as many of Thailand's vast industrial parks flooded. Likewise, large numbers of smaller Thai businesses either didn't have insurance or came to realize it was inadequate. The overarching financial health of international insurers became especially apparent. Local insurance brokers had been selling Thai policies on the cheap for years, without any serious due diligence on event probability. After the flood, many local insurers have stopped offering flooding policies. International insurers have pulled out of the market and foreign investors in Thailand's burgeoning export economy have made clear that the flooding is a liability they expect the government to take on board (e.g. Wright 2012). The government, in turn, has announced a $1.6 billion insurance pool offered to preclude foreign investors from moving production elsewhere. It is a clear case of climate risk arriving on the back of multiple inadequate infrastructures—urban, informational, capital asset—only to become a new liability of public funds in the context of global capital flows. The specificity of these climate vulnerabilities becomes apparent in the model event.

Model events do not establish a causal linkage to climate change. Rather, they ask how differently situated players are enabled to think about long-term climate vulnerabilities. Far from naturalizing climate change as a generic cause (i.e., separate from institutions, norms of social exclusion, specificities of capital and power through which a disaster arrives), in the Thai case I identify a complex problematization by Thais observing and participating from many different vantage points. For example, the decision-making of hydropower storage reservoir operators and managers of Bangkok's flood-gates was extensively debated in the press; debates about the politicization of flood control were widespread; and the government

response has been to bureaucratize flood management up to the highest level of government, with the Prime Minister presiding over two new water management bodies. In other words, whatever the climate impact, the proximate causes have been assigned as a matter of Thai responsibility over the not-natural, not-cultural contingencies pertaining to the specificity of an event. The model event makes it possible to ask whether situated practitioners are asking the right questions.

Climate vulnerabilities hinge not on a specific ontological conception of threat but on the transformation of pattern, and each of these terms invites a topological relation to planetary information (Blok 2011; Law and Mol 2001). For example, Paul Edwards writes of climate models "shimmering" with uncertainty (Edwards 2011: 337). "The past shimmers," he asks. "What about the future?" Data shimmering applies equally well to the oscillating presence and absence of summer Arctic ice minimums, with their apprehensive interpretability and the uncertain linkages to nonlinear geopolitical effects, as it does to the pulsating transformations of insect ecologies or the real time apprehension of flooding vulnerability.

One of the earliest modern scientific papers on climate change used a compelling methodology to identify "small but

persistent" biospheric changes (Keeling 1960, p. 1). Given the ongoing anxiety about scientific uncertainty, the challenge of how to think about small but persistent changes remains acute. For some, uncertainty means inaction is a legitimate response; for others, it allows imagination to run unchecked toward unnecessarily extreme assessments of impending doom. The fingerprint, bellwether and model event refute the idea that climate change narratives remain bound within the apocalyptic (Swyngedouw 2010). The world is not going to end, but neither will it stay the same due to a stroke of the pen on some international agreement. Rather, this grammar suggests a pragmatics of thinking through multiple possible futures. In different ways, these terms present an emerging vernacular adequate to the novel challenge of climate change, an informational event in which modeled and measured futures increasingly resonate with each other. ■

JEROME WHITINGTON *is a Research and Teaching Fellow at the National University of Singapore, where he is writing a book called* Accounting for Atmosphere: Human Climate Futures.

ACKNOWLEDGEMENTS Thanks to Chris Vasantkumar for a compelling discussion.

REFERENCES

Blok, Anders. 2011. "Topologies of Climate Change: Actor-network Theory, Relational-scalar Analytics, and Carbon-market Overflows," *Environment and Planning D: Society and Space* 28(5):896–912.

Boersma, P. Dee. 2008. "Penguins as Marine Sentinels" *BioScience* 58(7):597–607.

Collier, Stephen J., and Andrew Lakoff. 2008. The Vulnerability of Vital Systems: How "Critical Infrastructure" Became a Security Problem. In M. Dunn and K.S. Kristensen (eds.), *The Politics of Securing the Homeland: Critical Infrastructure, Risk and Securitisation*. London: Routledge.

Edwards, Paul 2011. *A Vast Machine*. Cambridge, MA: MIT Press.

Gramelsberger, Gabriele, and Johann Feichter. 2011. "Modelling the Climate System: An Overview," pp. 9–90 in *Climate Change and Policy*, DOI 10.1007/978-3-642-17700-2_2, Berlin: Springer-Verlag.

Huebert, Rob. et al. 2012. "Climate change & international security: The Arctic as a Bellwether." Arlington, Virginia: Center for Climate and Energy Solutions.

Karl, Thomas R., et al. 2008. Weather and Climate Extremes in a Changing Climate Final Report, Synthesis and Assessment Product 3.3. Washington D.C.: The U.S. Climate Change Science Program, Department of Commerce, NOAA National Climatic Data Center.

Keck, Frédéric. 2010. "Une sentinelle sanitaire aux frontiéres du vivant." *Terrain* 2010/1(54):27–41.

Keeling, Charles D. 1960. "The Concentration and Isotopic Abundances of Carbon Dioxide in the Atmosphere." *Tellus* VII.

Law, John, and Annemarie Mol. 2001. Situating Technoscience: An Inquiry into Spatialities. *Environment and Planning D: Society and Space* 19(5):609–621.

OED Online. 2012. "bell-wether, n." Oxford University Press. (accessed May 24, 2012).

Parmesan, Camille, and Gary Yohe. 2003. "A Globally Coherent Fingerprint of Climate Change Impacts Across Natural Systems." *Nature* 421(6918):37–42.

Swyngedouw, Erik. 2010. Apocalypse Forever? Post-political Populism and the Spectre of Climate Change. *Theory, Culture & Society* 27(2-3):213–232.

Wang, Muyin and James Overland. 2009. "A sea ice free summer Arctic within 30 years?", *Geophysical Research Letters*, 36(7):L07502, doi:10.1029/2009GL037820.

Whitington, Jerome. n.d. "Apprehension/Model Event: Speculative methodologies for Thai climate change flooding." Draft paper.

Wright, J. Nils. 2012. "Insurance capacity shrinks after Thai floods: Reinsurers pull back as businesses struggle to quantify losses," *Business Insurance*, 1 Jan 2012.

The scientist as sentinel

Climate scientists have a frightening message, but the public doesn't seem worried enough. **Naomi Oreskes** argues that the dispassionate ideal of science might be getting in the way.

SCIENTISTS HAVE BEEN WARNING THE WORLD for a long time about the risks of "dangerous anthropogenic interference in the climate system," but they also struggle with how to explain what that really means. People don't experience the climate system, people experience weather events. So it was perhaps inevitable that a day or two after "Superstorm" Sandy hit New York City, a journalist contacted me to ask if I thought Sandy would be a tipping point. Would this be the crucial event that convinced an otherwise skeptical American public that climate change is underway, and is, indeed, dangerous?

My immediate thought was that this event should be a tipping point, but whether it would be is another matter. Virtually as soon as the floodwaters stabilized in the subways, the usual cadre of self-proclaimed "skeptics" were spinning their usual arguments: that no one weather event proves systemic climate change.

These folks are formally correct, but then so was the tobacco industry when it insisted that no one lung cancer death proved smoking caused cancer. No one event proves climate change, because by definition climate is a pattern, and patterns can only be proved by, well, patterns. But every pattern is made up of individual contributions, and for some time now scientists have been seeing an emerging pattern of weather events consistent with what they have predicted. And while scientists in the 1960s could not explain why smoking caused the particular pattern of disease that it did, scientists today can explain why climate change is causing the observed pattern of extreme weather events. Carbon dioxide traps energy in the earth's atmosphere. That energy has to go somewhere, and one place it goes is into weather. Among other things, more energy in the system permits the development of more powerful storms. Storms are very dangerous. They kill people. They do billions of dollars in damage. They destroy cultural heritage and disrupt communities, sometimes permanently. Even when people re-build, their sense of safety and security is diminished. We saw this after Hurricane Katrina and we will be seeing it again in the weeks, months, and years to come as New York rebuilds after Superstorm Sandy.

SO WHY AREN'T MORE PEOPLE MORE AFRAID? Public opinion polls have consistently shown that only a small slice of American society is very worried about climate change, and less than half are even somewhat worried. Maybe we don't see the pattern. On my favorite radio station the commentator informs us each morning of the record high and low temperatures for that day. The record high is usually fairly recent—usually within the last thirty years and often within the last twenty—but the record lows are typically long ago, often fifty or even a hundred years. This is consistent with a warming trend. Yet the announcer never seems to notice... Fair enough. Most people are not poring over temperature records, much less analyzing them statistically to see if record highs are being broken more often these days than record lows. (They are.) But there seems to be a deeper problem.

If we take 1992—the year the United Nations Framework Convention on Climate Change was adopted—as a reasonable starting point when ordinary people paying a modicum of attention to public affairs would have learned that climate change posed a potential threat to human health and well-being as well as to other species—then we might expect that since then many people would have been at least somewhat worried. Two years before that, President George H.W. Bush—remembered by some as the President who did not know what a supermarket scanner was—told the press that "We all know that human activities are changing the atmosphere in unexpected and in unprecedented ways." Yet, despite knowing about the threat, and despite *seeing* ravaging floods, droughts, wildfires and now superstorms, only 20-30% of Americans over the past two decades have indicated to pollsters they were "quite concerned" about climate change. As of September 2012, only 36% thought that global warming is hurting people in the United States.[1]

Maybe this will change now, but maybe not. Certainly the harms are evident, but will people connect the harms to climate change? Will they see this as the "dangerous anthropogenic interference in the climate system" that our first President Bush promised to prevent? Perhaps, but perhaps not. Many thought Americans' attitudes towards climate change would change after Katrina, which remains the costliest event in U.S. history ($62 billion in insured damages, $1.25 trillion in overall losses, and 1,322 lives lost). They did, temporarily, but then seemed to settle back into the prior pattern of inattention. Reactions and responses to risk are obviously complex, and entail diverse and interacting social, political, cultural, economic and epistemic factors. But one element of climate change stands out as different from at least some other forms of risk addressed in this volume: the matter of who is trying to communicate the danger.

Fires are announced by fire alarms, a familiar presence in every school and public building. Earthquakes are generally 'announced' by the earthquakes themselves, when we feel our houses shake and see our windows rattle and even roll. Emerging epidemics get communicated largely by public health officials whose job it is to protect us from infectious diseases and other environmental pathogens. These officials take this aspect of their job seriously, and dedicate considerable attention to doing it effectively. (Whether they are successful is another matter.) Patients expect their doctors to alert them to less immediate health threats, and to try to persuade them to do something about them, whether it is quitting smoking, losing weight, or getting a flu shot. But communicating the risk of climate change falls not to familiar technological devices, immediate experience, doctors or public health officials, but to research scientists, mostly physical scientists. And this is a group singularly ill-equipped to communicate effectively to ordinary publics, particularly about issues that trigger alarm or fear.[2]

Consider this. Two years ago, I was on a panel at the American Geophysical Union with several extremely distinguished climate scientists. Everyone on the panel had the same message: Climate change is real, it is underway, and it is dangerous. During the question period, a woman stood up and said: "You are telling us that we have a very serious problem, but you don't *sound* at all worried. You don't even sound upset!"

She was right. The scientists in the room didn't sound worried. They certainly did not sound upset. And they almost never do. Because scientists take great pains in their work and demeanor to be rational, and scientists link rationality to dispassion. In my experience, scientists working on climate change consider it to be very important—indeed, crucial—to stay calm, to remain unemotional, and never, *ever*, get hysterical. In scientific circles, if you are emotional, it is assumed that you have lost your capacity to assess data calmly and therefore your conclusions become suspect. Robert Merton famously claimed that the norms of science were universalism, communism, organized skepticism, and disinterestedness, but he left out an important additional one: dispassion. Scientists can be counted on to stay calm and carry on. Or at least to try to.

In a recently published article my colleagues and I have shown

---

1. See (Leiserowitz et al. 2012). Ironically a recent report by Munich Re suggests that North America has been "particularly hard hit by weather catastrophes in recent years: Hurricane Katrina, tornadoes, floods, wildfires, searing heat and drought. The intensities of certain weather events in North America are among the highest in the world, and the risks associated with them are changing faster than anywhere else. They estimate over $1 trillion dollars in weather related damages (2011 dollars) and 30,000 lost lives during the period 1980-2011. They attribute the greater impact in North America to a combination of geographic and social factors. Geographically, "The North American continent is exposed to every type of hazardous weather peril—tropical cyclone, thunderstorm, winter storm, tornado, wildfire, drought and flood. One reason for this is that there is no mountain range running east to west that separates hot from cold air." Socially, North America is characterized by large population, urban sprawl, and high wealth, which makes damages relatively greater than they would be if the affected areas were poor (Re 2012).

2. There is a now a voluminous literature on communicating climate risk, and scientific societies have recently dedicated many conference panels to discussing the issue. Many of these efforts follow the deficit model of public understanding, suggesting that if only scientists explained the scientific evidence clearly, on a level that ordinary people could understand, then they accept and act upon it. This approach fails to acknowledge the deep social, cultural and economic interests that mitigate against action on the scale required, as well as the psychological reasons why people react to fear with anger, denial, and even violence. For entry into this literature, and a critique of why the deficit model is insufficient, see (Moser and Dilling 2004, Moser and Dilling 2007, and Boykoff 2010).

"You are telling us that we have a very serious problem, but you don't sound at all worried. You don't even sound upset!"

that scientists have systematically underestimated the threat of climate change. We suggest that they have done so for normative reasons: The scientific values of rationality, dispassion, and self-restraint lead them to demand greater levels of evidence in support of surprising, dramatic, or alarming conclusions than in support of less alarming conclusions. We call this tendency "erring on the side of least drama."

Climate change is very dramatic, and it is very worrisome. Superstorms, raving floods, devastating wildfires, not to mention ocean acidification and the threat it represents to the base of the food chain—are alarming. And scientists have terrible difficulty talking about them. It's not only that they err on the side of least drama in their conclusions, it's also that they *speak* without drama, even when their conclusions are dramatic. They speak without the emotional cadence that normal people expect to hear when someone is genuinely worried. So even when they are worried—and most climate scientists will tell you in private that they are—they just don't sound it.

How can you communicate danger without drama? How can you tell someone he or she should be worried when you don't sound worried yourself? How can you be a sentinel if you don't have a trumpet to blow, and wouldn't feel comfortable blowing it even if you did? ∎

NAOMI ORESKES *is Professor of History and Science Studies at the University of California, San Diego, and adjunct Professor of Geosciences at the Scripps Institution of Oceanography. Her most recent book, with co-author Erik Conway, is* Merchants of Doubt: How a Handful of Scientists Obscured the Truth on Issues from Tobacco Smoke to Global Warming *(Bloomsbury, 2010). It was awarded the Watson-Davis prize of the History of Science Society in 2012 and has appeared in Chinese, Japanese, Korean, French and German editions.*

BIBLIOGRAPHY

Boykoff, Maxwell T. 2011. *Who Speaks for the Climate?: Making Sense of Media Reporting on Climate Change.* Cambridge: Cambridge University Press.

Brysse, Keynyn, Naomi Oreskes, Jessica O'Reilly and Michael Oppenheimer, 2012. "Climate Change Prediction: Erring on the Side of Least Drama?" *Global Environmental Change,* 23(1):327–337.

Bush, George H.W. Speech at Georgetown University, 1990. http://www.youtube.com/watch?v=4Jnu09xQ4lk&noredirect=1

Leiserowitz, Anthony et al. (Yale Project on Climate Communication). 2012. Climate Change in the American Mind: Americans' Global Warming Beliefs and Attitudes in September 2012. Accessed at: http://environment.yale.edu/climate/item/Climate-Beliefs-September-2012

Meehl, Gerald A., Claudia Tibaldi, Guy Walton, David Easterling et al. 2009. Relative increase of record high maximum temperatures compared to record low minimum temperatures in the U.S. *Geophysical Research Letters* 36(23): L23701.

Moser, Susanne C. and Lisa Dilling. 2004. "Making climate hot: Communicating the urgency and challenge of global climate change." *Environment* 46(10):32–46 .

Moser, Susanne C. and Lisa Dilling. eds. 2007. *Creating a Climate for Change: Communicating Climate Change and Facilitating Social Change.* Cambridge; Cambridge University Press.

Munich Re. 2012. Severe Weather in North America. Accessed at: https://www.munichre.com/touch/naturalhazards/en/publications/weather_risks/issue/2012.aspx, see also, http://www.munichre.com/en/media_relations/press_releases/2012/2012_10_17_press_release.aspx.